The Phenomenal Power
of
Business Intelligence:
Managerial Skills
for the
21st Century

M.E. Burke,
Information Systems
Institute,
University of Salford

Europa Publications
Taylor & Francis Group plc

© Maria E. Burke 2003
Published by Europa Publications Limited 2003
11, New Fetter Lane
London EC4P 4EE
United Kingdom
(A member of the Taylor & Francis Group)

ISBN 0851424740

The Phenomenal Power

of

Business Intelligence:

Managerial Skills

for the

21st Century

M.E. Burke,

Information Systems

Institute,

University of Salford

Contents

Acknowledgements

I would like to thank those people who contributed to the compilation of this book. In particular, the authors of the case studies and the staff at the Chartered Management Institute and the Manchester Business School.

Towards the final completion of this book I took up my current position at the University of Salford's Information Systems Institute. However, most of this book was written whilst working with Manchester Metropolitan University and I would like to acknowledge this by thanking both my colleagues and students who provided much of the inspiration needed for a book of this kind. Finally I would like to extend sincere thanks to Sheila Webber for kindly acting as the reader of this text.

Introduction

The aim of the book is to raise awareness of the need to radically change management styles to fit in with the new patterns of working in the 21st century. There is a need for managers to reassess what skills are needed to manage those working remotely, using technology-centred communication to operate within a virtual organisation. Skills are also needed to analyse the impact of these changes on the structure of the organisation. However, it is almost impossible in a book of this nature to discuss every management theory and technique: those included here are those regarded as most appropriate and likely to be used regularly. The book is divided into eight chapters followed by three case studies. Each of the chapters provides ideas and discussion around the subject area and closes with an assessment of skills required by managers to manage situations in a creative and dynamic way.

The phenomenal power of business intelligence today is such that information is now pivotal to most organisations. The importance of a sound assessment of the external environment cannot be overemphasised and this area is considered in Chapter one. The internal environment, which needs to utilise all the information from the external environment, is another area in which business intelligence has gained in power. Indeed, organisational structures today are sometimes based around the pattern of information flows, and the impact of driving forces such as technology is examined in the second chapter. Chapter three deals with technology and its relationship to business organisations today. It traces the growth of technology, examines the current status of e-commerce and proposes a lifecycle model to assist with the analysis of the implementation of technology. The fourth chapter discusses business strategy, including the strategic analysis of the organisation and the place of knowledge management in strategic management. Chapter five examines the changing nature of marketing whilst Chapter six offers ideas for managing organisational relationships in the context of the changed environment. The concept of professionalism and how this is now an increasingly important issue due to the impact of new work patterns is discussed in Chapter seven. Finally, Chapter eight summarises the skills that have been discussed and places them into five different categories.

The case studies aim to provide simulated situations, which can be used to develop powers of analysis and encourage the reader to consider different ways management skills can be applied in business situations. The case studies differ in character and can be summarised as follows. Case study one concerns life in the student services department of a local college and deals with organisational problems. The second case study concerns a melancholic young man, not without a sense of humour, who finds himself in a difficult situation in his job at a local secondary school. The final case study concerns an industrial situation where there is a problem of communication and a complex ordering system, which almost leads to disaster.

This book is about the skills that will make a difference to the way in which businesses survive and flourish in this technological century. It is aimed primarily at students of business and management; practising managers who find themselves managing staff who work remotely; knowledge managers who wish to gain an insight into the general skills of managers and at all those with a thirst for knowledge and a willingness to consider new ideas about management skills.

The Phenomenal Power of Business Intelligence

Chapter 1

The external environment

Introduction

This chapter examines how organisations operate within the context of society as a whole – in the external environment. Businesses do not operate in a vacuum but are pulled and pushed by issues that occur everyday in our society. It is sometimes difficult to grasp exactly what these issues are as they can be hard to define. One way of overcoming this difficulty is to use a simple management classification that breaks down the issues into separate and clearly distinguishable factors: sociological, technological, economic, environmental and political (STEEP). Sociological factors refer to changes in demographics, consumer tastes, fashions and so on – in fact all the issues that reflect the nature of society. Technological factors include all aspects of new technology, the way in which the telecommunications industry is developing and the way technology can be applied to enhance business progress. Economic features include rates of inflation, interest rates and exchange rates, indeed all the factors that affect the general economic state of a particular country or economic bloc. Environmental issues reflect a concern for a safer, more eco-friendly world. Organisations reacted to this in various ways during the 1980s and 1990s, for instance, by the recycling of products and by using less packaging to sell products. Political factors include, for example, all decisions taken by local and national governments that affect the running of a business or an industry.

It is important to remember that none of the issues remains static: they are continually evolving and changing into new patterns. The external environment is the term used to refer to all the external factors that in some way can affect the running of the business.

This chapter is divided into four sections, which are concerned with recent major changes in the external environment. The first section examines the concept of change and the second section looks at major shifts in the way in which organisations operate – in particular the different forms of organisational hierarchies that have developed over recent years. The third section relates to changes in work patterns and the final section suggests some new models of the skills required to manage the external environment effectively in the 21st century. Finally, when considering the challenges of the external environment it is important to remember that it is humans who inevitably and permanently play the role of lifetime members of society, and who in turn influence the complex issues that become our ever-changing external environment.

The concept of change

The way in which technology has developed during the last 10 years has radically affected the way in which businesses operate. For example, most businesses now use technology not just as a way of helping organisations to run more efficiently but also as part of the interface of selling products (and services) to the consumer. An example of this is the increasing use of the Internet as a selling outlet for products, hence the creation of e-business (literally meaning business conducted electronically). Other frequently used terms are on-line business and e-commerce, both referring to business conducted electronically, usually via the Internet.

The rise of companies conducting business in this way is phenomenal and has given way to another relatively new term – dot.com companies. This phrase originally referred to the Internet address of any Internet company and consisted of a company name followed by a full stop and the word com (company), for instance, soap.com. The term today tends to have a more generic sense, meaning all companies that transact business over the Internet.

E-business is becoming increasingly prevalent as a method of doing business, as society becomes more familiar with technological products. For example, the use of email, mobile phones, home computers, laptops and Internet access are now almost everyday items and services for a large part of society. How then has the use of new technology changed the way in which businesses are able to operate? Business transactions have become faster – resulting in competition becoming fiercer, which in turn results in more firms merging as weak organisations can no longer compete in this new, hard, sharp, technologically driven world. Finally, any sense of certainty and stability regarding a firm's external environment is no longer apparent – instead the environment is filled with constant changes and shifts, which organisations must recognise in order to exploit business opportunities to the best advantage.

During 2000 the UK government responded to these changes and created new policies, which aim to encourage businesses to use the new technologies fully. Indeed, for the first time the government set up an office within the Department of Trade and Industry (DTI) whose remit is to co-ordinate e-business strategies. This has been achieved by the appointment of a Minister for Small Firms and E-business together with the appointment of an E-envoy. In addition, the government is working on draft editions of documents that aim to modernise government bureaucracy through the use of new technology.

The DTI has created an initiative, 'Business in the Information Age', which includes the following areas:

*   information on general guidance and advice
*   information on electronic trading internationally
*   marketing information regarding the 'information age' in general
*   sources of funding and support for technology development
*   information security
*   the future of e-business.

Details of all these initiatives can be found on the DTI web site whose address is given at the end of this chapter. While all of these areas are relevant and of great interest to the information industry, the final category – the future of e-business – is worthy of further examination here.

The future of e-business is considered by task forces and panels of experts within three arenas:

- *The 'DTI Future Unit'* This unit has been established to create insights into industries and markets of the future.

- *The 'DTI Knowledge 2000' conference* This provided an opportunity for examination of the new knowledge-based economy and created a forum for discussion of ideas and suggestions. The conference may become a regular annual event.

- *The 'DTI Foresight's e-commerce task force'* This panel has been established to determine the impact that electronic commerce will have on business models by the year 2010.

The DTI's Foresight e-commerce task force produced a consultation report, *Smoke on the Water: Fire in the Sky*, details of which are available on the DTI web site. After some consideration the task force arrived at the conclusion that those organisations that achieve success in the e-business world will be characterised by the following factors.

- The value of the business will derive from culture and knowledge rather than products.

- Competitors will find it hard to copy the methods used to create this value.

- Businesses will be able to manage the more dynamic and flexible relationships that characterise the electronic economy better.

- Businesses will help their workforce develop the skills they need to use digital content, services and systems fully.

In order for organisations to achieve these characteristics the task force identified three target areas:

- an open and accessible society (labelled by the DTI as the need for a confident society)

- investment in skills and the emerging e-business areas (labelled by the DTI as the need for an energised society)

- quicker response to business needs by the government, the need for privacy and trust issues to be addressed and recognition of the fact that different educational approaches are required (labelled by the DTI as being about the active consumer and the interactive citizen.)

The authors of the report closed by commenting on the need for appropriate skills in this new age. 'The skills to deal with the online world are skills for life, not just work. The present (educational) model of daily attendance at a single location will change.'[1] This conclusion emphasises the need to manage change and develop skills not just in an ad-hoc, piecemeal way but by taking a planned, rounded, holistic approach to the whole area of training.

The need to manage change that will create the government ideal of an energised, confident society, filled with active consumers and interactive citizens in an effective way has never been more important. Taken at its most fundamental level the changes are about the successful management of change and it is the way in which change is managed that we will now examine. In order to manage change properly it is essential first to identify the skills and qualities that managers need to undertake this task.

In 1971 Livingstone argued that three qualities are associated with successful managers.[2]

- *The need for power* Good managers have a need to influence others. To do this they do not rely on the authority of their positions but on their superior knowledge and skill.

- *The need to manage* Only those people who want to affect the performance of others and who derive satisfaction when they do so are likely to become effective managers.

- *The capacity for empathy* The effective manager needs the ability to understand and cope with the often expressed emotional needs of others in the organisation in order to win their co-operation.

From this basic classification we can start to build up a picture of the qualities called for in successful managers if businesses are to thrive in the 21st century:

- superior knowledge and skill

- understanding

- the ability to foster co-operation in others

- the ability to engender in others the sense of working as a team.

So, even in the early 1970s when this work was undertaken the 'softer' skills of management had been identified as one of the keys of successful management. Yet we are now living in the 21st century, a time that may in the future be known as the century when technology and information combined to make our lives – and in particular our business practices – smarter and more effective. What then are the implications of the identification of 'soft' management skills for this century? In order to answer this we need to step back and examine the changes that have taken place during the last 20 years. Eryn Brown, writing

11

during the late 1990s, noted the changes in the size of companies, job creation and security, working standards, loyalty of employers and at organisational hierarchy levels.[3] All of these changes require the 'softer' skills of management to implement a sense of ownership of the organisation's true mission. In particular, it is changes to organisational hierarchy levels that have most significance regarding changes to working lives and our external environment. Organisational structures will thus be examined in the next section.

Changing organisations

The changes in the way in which many organisations have been structured in the past 10 to 15 years (into flat, fluid, flexible structures) show a radical departure from the old-fashioned, rigid, top-heavy pyramid styles of yesterday. Many of the original theories about organisational structures were developed during the early part of the 20th century when the nature of society differed considerably from today. It is outside the remit of this book to discuss organisational theory in depth, but for detail on the history and evolution of organisational theory the classic work edited by D.S. Pugh is highly recommended.[4] For the purposes of this book, however, we need to consider the prospects of the organisations of the future. Management scholars writing as far back as 1988 identified the future of organisations as being information based. 'The typical business will be knowledge based, an organisation composed largely of specialists who direct and discipline their own performance through organised feedback from colleagues customer and headquarters.'[5] Many are likely to become learning organisations – ones in which individual needs are increasingly met through an emphasis on self-development as well as formal training.

Organisations must reflect the current external environment – their social, technological, economic and political climate. The research undertaken in this area by Burns and Stalker identified five different kinds of environment, from stable to least predictable, and within these they distinguished between the mechanistic and the organic systems of management.[6] The mechanistic system is appropriate to a stable environment and is characterised by factors such as specialisation of tasks, hierarchical structure designed to control, insistence on loyalty to managers and knowledge and prestige attached to those near the top of the hierarchy. The organic system of management is much more suited to the fluid and changing conditions of today and is characterised by the contribution of special knowledge to the task – the adjustment of individual tasks through interaction with others, a network structure of control and authority, and a commitment to the progress of the organisation. It is this system that seems to be the one with most relevance for today's changing and fluid external environment.

One of Drucker's criteria for an effective organisation structure is that it must be organised for business performance.[7] If this key function is somehow lost in the detail and the upheaval of the change then failure in the medium to long term is almost guaranteed. Organisations that do not alter are unlikely to prosper, resulting in weak, unsuccessful businesses, either ripe for take-over or that will eventually become so outdated that they begin to fail, cease to be competitive and are unable to function.

The younger the organisation the more likely it is to be smaller and to fit into today's high-tech IT world of flat structures, increased team working and temporary project groups. However, when introducing – or evaluating – any major change there are three important questions to be asked in the quest for organisational effectiveness.

- What effect does the change or restructuring have on the information flow in the organisation?

- In what ways will tasks change – and how will this affect staff and staff morale?

- How will the restructure affect the culture of the organisation?

These three areas of information flow, staff and culture change all have a significant role to play in the enhancement of organisational performance. How then are the new organisational designs classified? Recent research by Travica suggests that the new organisational designs can be characterised in four ways: as organic, as adhocracies, as networked or as virtual.[8] Organic organisations change and redefine themselves according to individual tasks. In an adhocracy the organisation is characterised by low formalisation of behaviour, lack of standardisation and clear role definition. Networked organisations have overlapping managerial responsibilities, vague roles and the potential for conflict. Virtual organisations tend to produce a product that is customised to the individual consumer. Travica continues his work by identifying a 'five-f method', which characterises the non-traditional organisation – flexible, fluid, fickle, fit and free. A notable element is the way in which the 'softer' skills are still taking precedence in management theory and in organisational theory.

The newest organisational designs are those inherent in on-line businesses. Tapscott identified five emergent business systems – agora, aggregation, alliance, value chain and distribution networks.[9] These can be defined as follows.

- *The agora business system* This is an electronic market driven by competitive pricing in a business-to-business environment. Information is the key to these markets.

- *The aggregation business model* An example of this is the electronic megastore, which offers access to a wide range of goods combined with delivery to customers. It is usually identified as a business-to-consumer market and success depends on effective delivery. As above, access to good quality, accurate information is the key factor.

- *The alliance business system* This is a loose affiliation of individuals around a service offer. Stakeholders and sympathetic individuals or organisations are connected together, which creates the value. The alliance then creates intellectual value and communication becomes the key factor.

- *The value chain model* This is the use of management of information systems by manufacturers to build specific products for individual customers to construct a chain. The value comes from communication with the customer and the supplier network. Again, communication seems to be the key factor.

- *The distributive network model* This is the exchange of information among the creator's users and customers. This reduces service costs at one level but may increase the complexity of calls and queries.

Not all companies fit neatly into individual categories – some fit into part of one, some have departments that may fit into several of these areas. Most Internet companies are still evolving and changing and will probably continue to do so for some time. However, this work helps us to identify how the new on-line business world is growing and what skills are going to be needed to manage the information industry in the future.

Changing work patterns

There are now various guides that offer advice to managers on new, flexible working arrangements.[10] These include flexible working hours, reduced hours, breaks from employment and teleworking. Research into these changes has revealed some interesting developments. For example, studies such as those by Cooper have concentrated on the psychological implications of the changing patterns of work.[11] Cooper's research found that work trends include more flexible and home-based work, less security, constant change and longer working hours. The importance of quality of life was also apparent. In order to be successful managers need to be aware of these psychological changes and plan motivation strategies accordingly. There is now a variety of terms used to describe different work patterns. For example, the term portfolio careers – where people work for different organisations and carry out different tasks for each – is becoming used increasingly in everyday language. Butler and Waldroop stated that the solution to recruitment problems is to match jobs to deeply embedded life interests.[12] This technique is known as job sculpting. A prevalent term in the United States is that of contingent workers – where workers are on short-term contracts in order to increase flexibility in the organisation. The term virtual workplace is also increasing in use to identify new, high-tech, remotely linked office spaces. In all these new forms of work pattern there is a need to be able to identify and consider work design, skills, competencies and rewards. All of these need careful consideration and planning by astute, up-to-date managers.

Pugh's work on change management in the information arena makes salient points about the nature of modern information services.[13] He identified the following factors as being the driving forces towards change and changing work patterns:

- the breakdown of consensus about how the information industry is defined

- uncertainty caused by the above debate

- cross-disciplinary collaboration

- differentiation between sectors and marked contrasts between some internal and external environments

- new experts – the key IT and related skills of the (newly) trained generation of the information profession

- entrepreneurism – sometimes difficult to sell to established staff in the traditional roles

- competition from other experts and from users who no longer need the interface of the information professional.

All these factors need to be accounted for when considering what new skills are needed to manage the new work patterns in order to move forward and embrace the challenge of the 21st century.

What skills are required to manage the external environment?

What skills are required to enable today's managers and information professionals to deal effectively with the external environment? Research carried out for the Institute of Management found that there had been a clear move in the last few years towards formal and more specific training for managers.[14] The skills found to be most needed in order to ensure good management practice across the organisation were management of people, leadership, team working and a focus on the customer. In a similar vein, work undertaken by Skelton and Abell identified a way of perceiving 'skills gaps' in both managers and employees by the use of a model which combines knowledge roles and key skill sets[15].

Models regarding skills then need to be redesigned and developed for the 21st century. The three skills that managers need to meet the challenges of the external environment are an awareness of change, the need for flexibility and being open to new attitudes. These key skills are discussed below.

An awareness of change in the external environment can be gained by reading relevant professional literature. However, by reading wide and sometimes non-relevant material regarding changes in many different industries a new extended kind of awareness can be created. In addition, an awareness of some kinds of forecasting is an excellent tool when trying to chart the potential changes within the external environment. For example, the skills needed in scenario forecasting, such as tracking, scanning and searching for significant signals that may be a sign of the beginning of a trend, are now essential tools that can be used in order to sharpen up the competitive edge of a business.[16] The established terms for the traditional forms of these skills can perhaps now be recrafted into terms that are more appropriate for the 21st century. An awareness of change can thus be remodelled into the need for alertness.

The need for flexibility, showing a knowledge and acceptance of new forms of working and new attitudes to work, can sometimes present particular difficulties for the manager working in a large, traditional organisation who is acting as the interface between what the organisation requires and what may be needed by staff – which may be very different. There are three potential solutions to this difficulty. The first is to find some kind of compromise between what the organisation requires and what staff require. But this solution will always be full of tension and emotional turmoil and will almost inevitably take a good portion of a manager's time trying to organise a situation that will satisfy most of the people for most of the time. The second solution is to educate those at the top of the organisation and attempt to change the situation from within by forming new policies that are more in line with staff needs, but that also fulfil the needs of the organisation. This is a long-term solution and will take time and bravery to implement. The third solution takes both the first two solutions to their logical conclusion: if the organisation cannot or will not adapt and adopt to new flexible working practices eventually staff will leave, recruitment will become more difficult, and the reputation of the organisation will suffer. The result of this could be that the organisation will no longer survive, as it will be unable to compete. There is also a danger that another organisation will take over or merge with the organisation in question and so the separate distinguishable identity of that particular organisation could be lost forever.

The need for knowledge and acceptance of new working practices can thus be seen to be of paramount importance. The term that perhaps most closely describes this skill is an ability to be open-minded about work practices.

Focus on the end game – this is the term used to describe the ultimate aim, the reason for managing, which is usually to improve organisational effectiveness in order to increase profit or give a better level of service. Managers need to have one clear aim; the danger is that because they are dealing with many different and complex issues the real aim of good management practice becomes clouded. A way to avoid this is to try to be one step ahead of the competition by always focusing on the end game. The skill could be known as an awareness of current attitude change but this in itself is not really enough – the point is always to 'win' by keeping aware of changes and attitudes and to focus one's mind on the end game – whatever that may be. No doubt the influences of the external world will twist and turn in all directions and sometimes be very difficult to define, but it is a vital skill for a good manager to be able to identify these changes, plan reaction to the changes, implement the plans and re-evaluate the situation in order to meet fully the challenges of the external environment.

References

1. DTI. *Smoke on the Water: Fire in the Sky*. Foresight: e-commerce task force consultation paper. London: DTI, 2000

2. Livingstone, J.S. 'The myth of the well educated manager', *Harvard Business Review* 49(1), 1971, pp. 79–89

3. Brown, E. 'Big business meets the e-world', *Fortune International, ed.* 140(9), 8 November 1999, pp. 62–5, 68–9, 72

4. Pugh, D.S. *Organisation Theory: Selected Readings*. London: Penguin, 1971

5. Little, B. 'New world order', *Management Skills and Development* Oct–Nov 1998, pp. 24–7

6. Burns, T and Stalker, G. *The Management of Innovation*. London: Tavistock, 1966

7. Drucker, P.F. 'The coming of the new organisation', *Harvard Business Review* 66(1), 1988, pp. 45–53

8. Travica, B. *New Organisational Designs: Information Aspects*. Stamford, CT: Ablex Publishing, 1999

9. Tapscott, D. 'Five emergent business systems', *Smoke on the Water: Fire in the Sky*. Foresight: e-commerce task force consultation paper. London: DTI, 2000

10. New Ways to Work Company. *Time for Change – a Guide to Work Patterns for Small and Medium sized Enterprises*. London: NWWC, 1999

11. Cooper, C. 'The psychological implications of the changing patterns of work', *RSA Journal* 45(5484), 1998, pp. 74–80

12. Butler, T. and Waldroop, J. 'Job sculpting: the art of retraining our best people', *Harvard Business Review* 77(5), 1999, pp. 144–52

13. Pugh, L. *Change Management in Information Services*. Aldershot: Gower, 2000

14. Institute of Management. *Achieving Management Excellence: a Survey of UK Management Development at the Millennium* by Chris Mabey and Andrew Thomson of the Open University Business School in association with the Department for Education and Employment and the Department of Trade and Industry, 2000

15. Skelton, V and Abell, A. *Developing Skills for Information in the Knowledge Ecomony*. London: TFPL, 2001

16. Burke, M. 'Scenario forecasting the role of the business information professional', *Business Information Review* 11(1), 1994, pp. 34–9

Web sites

DTI – *www.dti.gov.uk/infoage/index.htm*

Foresight – *www.foresight.gov.uk*

Chapter 2

The internal environment

Introduction

The term internal environment refers to all business matters contained within the boundaries of an organisation. This can include such factors as the formulation of goals, the determination of objectives, the creation of policy, the implementing of policy, the goal outputs – and some form of performance measurement of the goals. The character of the internal environment is shaped by the way in which information flows around the organisational structure and by the information resources and systems used by the organisation. However, the internal environment is inevitably influenced by the forces that shape the external environment and these forces can be referred to as the driving forces of the internal environment. The aim of this chapter is to examine how organisations operate their internal environment to optimise best performance.

The chapter is divided into five sections, which examine various facets of the internal environment. The first section examines the structural design of organisations and the second identifies the driving forces of the internal environment. The third section deals with the information flows and information patterns within an organisation. The fourth section looks briefly at the information systems that are used to control and shape the internal environment and the final section identifies the new skills that are required to manage this environment.

The structural design of organisations

One way in which the internal environment can be wholly influenced is by the way in which the organisational structure is designed. The perennial question in this area is whether the function of an organisation can influence the structure of the organisation. In order for us to decide what skills are needed for managers in this area we need as much information as possible about the nature of organisations.

According to Tushman and Nadler, 'The generally accepted view of organisational design that has evolved is that the structure of an organisation should match or fit characteristics of certain variables both inside and outside the organisational system.'[1] They continue by commenting about the main question in design, which has been to identify variables that will enable researchers to make consistent and valid predictions of what kinds of organisational structures will be most effective in different situations. Another important finding from their work is the classification of assumptions about how organisations function. Here is a brief summary of these assumptions.

- Organisations are open social systems, which need to deal with areas of uncertainty. In order to manage external and internal areas of uncertainty, organisations must develop information processing mechanisms.

- Organisations can be viewed as information processing systems in order to facilitate the effective collection, processing and distribution of information.

- Organisations can also be broken down and viewed as a set of sub-organisations or divisions and departments. It is important to examine the best design of each division rather than the whole design of the entire structure.

These theories were proposed in 1978 and much work has been done in this area since then. However, for our purposes we need to compare how these ideas have been affected by changes up to 2003.

- *Organisations as open social systems dealing with areas of uncertainty* Areas of uncertainty have increased to the point where there are no longer any areas of solid facts. Change is so vast and all encompassing that organisations have had to find new ways of managing the information – hence the rise in popularity of knowledge management.

- *Organisations as information processing systems* These systems have been radically affected by the development in telecommunications and technology. Information systems are designed specifically to assist with this role.

- *Organisations as subsets* Because the nature of work has changed so radically organisations have had to become much more task-orientated.

Two other assumptions derived from recent work developments are that there are no longer any set patterns of working and that technology is now a major driving force. However, it must be noted that while such theories can aid organisational design they cannot 'guarantee organisational success due to the fact that the effectiveness of a structure is fundamentally determined by the uncontrollable elements of human nature'.[2]

Is organisational design really about flexible restructuring to fit the function of the organisation? If so, then management of the internal organisation must be about the management of change.

The driving forces of the internal environment

The driving forces of an organisation are the factors that pull and push an organisation into a certain pattern. They are usually opposing forces and the organisation has to position itself in a way that balances the forces and ensures that it is in a position of some control.

What used to be known as information technology (IT) is one of the most powerful forces that affect an organisation. This has now developed to such an extent and had such a wide-ranging impact on communications that the term IT is no longer appropriate to describe the way in which we use technology in the 21st century. The term information and communications technology (ICT) now more accurately describes the way in which IT is used in organisations today.

What factors drive the technology and therefore the information systems of an organisation? In order to answer this question we need to take a step back and examine the initial IT patterns of the late 20th century. In the late 1980s Maddison listed the factors that drove the broad pattern of the use of IT:[3]

- an organisation's constant need to improve and evolve
- the human and social factors resulting from IT leading to changing methods of working
- the fact that IT products change, grow and improve in performance and accessibility
- the pressure of IT producers
- the growth of specialist skills
- the growth and changes in organisations.

It is now possible to take a second look at these factors and apply them to life in 2003. In this way it is possible to establish how these particular driving forces have changed and evolved into new patterns.

- An organisation's constant need to improve and evolve is especially relevant in the rapidly changing world of the 21st century. Many new types of organisations are developing with different forms of structures from those seen in the past.

- The human and social factors resulting from IT have led to more flexible ways of working due to the development of fast, effective telecommunications. The increase in remote methods of working has had an impact on the way in which managers are able to motivate – and indeed manage – the human resource in general.

- The growth in IT products, improvements in performance and accessibility have made IT one of the most powerful of all the driving forces. The new technology available in 2003 is increasingly able to link together different modes of communications. For instance, the use of Wireless Application Protocol (WAP) on mobile telephones has enabled email and text messages to be received in increasingly portable ways. Other examples include the enabling of email and Internet access through various access routes.

- The pressure of IT producers has resulted in increasingly fierce competition. In addition, pricing issues and product performance have become even more competitive. The problem of a few large companies dominating the industry has been recognised and this may lead to yet another shift in industry patterns in the near future.

- The growth of specialist skills is very relevant in 2003; there is a crucial need for all employees to have the skills necessary to navigate the new ICT systems. Education at primary school level is changing as children become computer literate at a very early age. In addition most organisations have now recognised the need for continual training in this area.

- The 21st century has also seen growth and change in organisations, from the traditional hierarchical pyramid to flatter and more streamlined structures. Also of note is the growth of the multinationals – and the power with which they can dominate a particular industry.

It can be seen, then, that all these pressures form the driving forces of the internal environment as each of the factors affect the working conditions and the culture within the organisations. The driving forces themselves, however, can only be successfully managed if the organisation has devised successful methods of controlling the way in which information flows within the organisational structure.

Information flows and information patterns within an organisation

Information can be said to flow either vertically or horizontally through an organisation. These types of information flows are important for different reasons and need to be carefully managed both as separate entities and in combination. It is also essential to co-ordinate carefully the way in which technology is used to control the systems.

Horizontal information flows can be defined as information that passes between divisions and crosses the boundaries of the managerial reporting structure. Thus the information that flows vertically across the organisation is used to control the various functions of an organisation. Vertical information flows, however, should map onto the structure of the organisation through which they flow. The information normally flows from the managers at the top of the organisation down to all the middle managers and central sections and then towards the bottom of the organisation. In an ideal world the flow of information should be in both directions – up and down the organisation.

However, there are three problems with this type of information flow. First, at each level of the structure the information can be changed or filtered (either deliberately or by accident); thus what may have started out as clear information at the top may result in confused messages at lower levels in the organisation. The second problem with the vertical information flow is that information can be regarded by some members of the organisation as a crucial 'power source'. The fact that managers (and employees) are able in some way to control data may give some of them a sense of power, which cannot be overlooked. The information can then be used to play political games within the organisation. This skilful playing – and winning – of organisational games can be of vital importance, and success may lie in having the ability to analyse the games of others and manipulate a situation so that the driving forces are turned in favour of a particular organisation. The third problem with vertical information flows is that there is little sharing of information between sub-units in the organisation as the flow does not move horizontally. This can then cause problems of ineffective communication.

The impact of new technology on information flows has been that the manager no longer has the power to store or release information, the messages are no longer subject to confusion and the staffing structure of the organisation may also be subject to change. Most organisations today already have some kind of basic computerised information system. However, as technology becomes increasingly advanced and more embedded in the structure of the organisation a strategy must be prepared that allows a new organisation (and its employees) to evolve and adapt to the new internal environment.

As organisations grow in size and complexity the need for strict control of information in order to provide a service or manufacture a product within exact specifications is increasing. Thus the need for more tightly controlled and co-ordinated information systems becomes a major requirement and investment of most organisations.

Information systems used to control and shape the internal environment

Design of the internal environment is something that is often ignored as mangers tend to concentrate on balancing the external pressures and everyday administration – but there is a way in which the organisation can both design the internal environment and exert some influence on the position of the organisation. This can be achieved by the carefully planned implementation and execution of the organisation's information system.

The key questions to consider when considering and planning a new information system are:

- What are the information requirements of the organisations?
- What is the present strategy of the organisation?
- What are the future plans of the organisation in terms of the product strategy?
- What training schemes are available for present and future staff?
- What are the staff working patterns?

31

As organisations develop tasks become more project-orientated and employees work either as individuals or in teams. Establishment of the pattern of work is a vital area, which needs close monitoring in terms of the changing information needs. When designing an information system flexibility and a thorough and accurate knowledge of the plans and workings of the organisation are essential – all the information systems must be able to adapt to change rapidly. Control of the internal environment becomes increasingly important in order to provide some form of stability to the organisation.

What skills are required to manage the internal environment?

What new skills are required for the manager of the internal environment in the 21st century? The main points seem to be the change from a reasonably static and stable environment to management of a more fluid and flexible one, which moves continually along a spectrum but never anchors in any one place.

Control of this new environment requires some new skills combined with more traditional management ones, such as:

- the ability to establish design structures that fit both the internal and the external environment
- effective communication with information systems teams
- the establishing of new roles as designers of organisational structures
- the ability to be flexible

- the ensuring of good control of knowledge management at all levels in the organisation

- astute powers of analysis in order to create the appropriate internal environment

- the ability to manage within a continual shifting of patterns rather than a stable environment.

Control of the internal environment is possible but it must happen in harmony with the external environment. It is a manager's task constantly to monitor the internal environment and to ensure that all members of the organisation are kept aware of changes. The technology exists to ensure that this can happen, for instance, through intranets, which can be updated frequently. Technology, new systems and skills can be used to push organisations further forward, ready to respond to life in the future.

References

1. Tushman, M.L. and Nadler, D.A. 'Information processing as an integrating concept in organisational design', *Academy of Management Review* July 1978, pp. 613–24

2. Burke, M and Tulett, K. 'Impact of information needs on organisational design', *Journal of the American Society for Information Science* 50(4), 1999, pp. 380–1

3. Maddison R. 'The management of information systems'. In *Information Systems and IT for Managers*. Milton Keynes: Open University Press, 1989

The Phenomenal Power of Business Intelligence

Chapter 3

Technology and business

Introduction

Can business survive without the employment of technology? To answer this question we need to take a historical perspective on business trading. Trading used to be primarily local but as the transport infrastructure developed and improved it became national. Then as flights and sea passages became safer and more accessible trade slowly became international. Trade was considered so important in the 15th and 16th centuries that many voyages were commissioned to find new markets in the form of continents discovered by explorers such as Columbus, Magellen and Vasco da Gama. These new countries then formed what came to be known, during that period, as the 'New World'. Today, our 'New World' has been created by moves towards freedom and harmony. Trade between countries and continents is freer now than it has ever been before. This is in part due to the changes that have taken place at the end of the 20th century, such as the success of the European Union in removing trade barriers between EU member countries, the collapse of the Soviet bloc, the rise of multinational companies and the developments in trade communications and technology. International trade today is vital to the success of all our countries.

The aim of this chapter is to examine the intricate relationship between two important areas – technology and business. This is achieved by looking at recent developments in technological development, the problems and opportunities of e-commerce, ideas for bringing some form of order to the chaos, issues around technology and leadership and the skills required for managing the relationship between business and technology in the 21st century.

Recent developments in technological development

During the 1960s and 1970s computers became widespread in most business organisations. Initially they were used to take the boredom and frustration out of repetitive tasks. Inevitably some employees lost jobs or were redeployed elsewhere in the organisation, resulting in general backlash and fear of computers replacing people. However, as the decades progressed the technology developed and was used for other tasks, which made jobs easier, the work more efficient and enhanced the reputation of the organisation as being at the 'cutting edge' and 'embracing the latest technology'. By the time technology was widely accepted as a way of life in business corporations technology had also been accepted in society. Universities and colleges recognised the need for new skills and proceeded to design and offer new technology courses as new skills were required in the marketplace. Gradually information technology courses became combined with business and so business technology courses were created.

In the 1990s the use of the Internet became widespread. At first it was employed by a few people but gradually its ease of use resulted in increasing popularity. As the Internet and web sites become more and more familiar society is witnessing acceptance of the Internet as a potential for increasing business. Many companies are now exploring how they can exploit the Internet as another way of accessing customers – almost as an addition to their distribution channel.

This exploration of new ways of doing business then led to new terms being developed – rather than the cumbersome phrase 'doing business on the Internet' the term electronic commerce or (e-commerce) was born. At the start of the 21st century this seems to be one of the most popular ways of exploiting the power of the Internet in order to gain access to customers, to inform customers about products and to demonstrate how modern and up to date a company is in terms of its use of technology.

The UK government is pushing business to use and exploit technology in order to increase the competitiveness of UK industry. However, estimates about uptake of e-commerce have tended to be based on PC usage, yet there is an increasing trend for consumers to use other devices such as the television set as the main portal for access to the Internet. This is significant in that it is difficult to establish an accurate picture of the uptake of e-commerce at the time of writing (2003).

At the birth of this new century we are now witnessing two distinct factors – the increasing use of more portable technology and the levelling out of the playing fields regarding the way technology is being used to gain competitive advantage. However, the virtual world is not yet a world of certainty. Indeed, virtual investment in Internet companies failed spectacularly towards the end of the year 2000 – almost as a parallel of the South Sea Bubble in the days of new discoveries. Yet there can be social benefits from failure, as can be seen from this description of a comparison of failed Internet companies with the development of the electricity industry in 1890:

> *John Lerner, Professor of Business Administration at Harvard Business School, draws an analogy with the development of the electricity industry in the 1890s when hundreds of companies sprang up with ideas for exploiting the new technology and raised money on the public markets. Many of the companies went for models that were not successful – but even for projects that turned out to be classed as failures there could still be a substantial social return because they led to an even greater understanding of what business models did and did not work.*[1]

Thus technology can benefit all aspects of society. The next development has been that of e-commerce and this is examined in the next section.

E-commerce – a land of problems and opportunities

Although e-commerce is hailed as the way forward for business, are the expectations of e-commerce unrealistic? Although many companies are taking up the option of conducting business electronically, others are still hesitant.

There are many studies about the UK market for e-commerce, such as that undertaken by the Retail and Consumer Services Foresight Panel about the future of retailing in an e-commerce world.[2] The findings of this report are very interesting and the full text can be accessed on line at the address given at the end of this chapter. The results concerning the advantages of e-commerce included the following benefits.

Benefits to retailers are:

- extended opening times in all time zones in the world
- the ability to rapidly alter information on product specifications
- facilitated access to niche and overseas customers
- customer involvement in product and service innovations
- increased customer loyalty
- level playing fields
- increased profitability (reduced support costs and costs per transactions)
- provision of accurate data to enhance stock management.

Benefits to the consumer are:

- accurate product information
- ease of comparison shopping
- immediate delivery of certain products
- reduced costs (electronically open marketplace).

However, if predictions are accurate and retail e-commerce becomes a way of life then the movement of goods can still be seen to be a practical difficulty today. The logistics of the entire population buying goods via the e-commerce route and having them delivered to the door results in practical problems of parking, loading and unloading at convenient moments and delivering goods when people are expecting them. The delivery infrastructures to back up retail e-commerce can still be seen as very problematic.

In 1999, Allcock and others examined barriers to the use of the Internet, in particular for information seeking.[3] The key obstacles they identified were:

- technical barriers (such as viruses, speed of searches, search technique problems – which search engines to use to best effect)
- physical problems concerning lack of time
- lack of access; changes in personnel
- Internet service provider problems
- site design and the lack of staff training.

Other research undertaken in the following year[4] found the top 10 barriers to e-commerce to be:

- security
- trust and risk
- lack of qualified personnel
- lack of business models
- culture
- user authentication and lack of public infrastructure
- organisation
- fraud and risk of loss
- the Internet or Web is too slow and not dependable
- legal issues.

It is interesting to note which barriers appear in both lists. The two major common issues are concerns about the lack of qualified personnel and changes in personnel, and the speed of access to some Internet pages.

Other results from the second study showed that there were problems with managing technological and organisational change. So, how are the managers who are in the middle of new technology able to impose some sense of structure on these problems and opportunities?

Creating order from chaos

Order must be created from the chaotic relationship between business and technology – from the constant pulling and pushing within the organisation's internal and external environment. It may be helpful for companies dealing with this issue to use a set of questions based loosely around practical, 'soft' or organisational issues, to check out the respective advantages of using the latest technology or e-commerce methods (or both) in selling more products.

Practical issues include:

- security
- the Internet being too slow and speed of access to pages
- legal matters
- fraud and risk of loss
- user authentication.

'Soft' issues include:

- trust of employees versus risk of abuse of the system
- lack of qualified personnel.

Organisational issues include:

- lack of (proven) business models
- organisational problems
- structural problems.

When these criteria are grouped together it becomes clear that the life cycle of the implementation of technology and exploitation of e-commerce must follow a set pattern based around these issues but starting from the initial 'adoption of an idea' stage (see Figure 1). These stages are: adoption of the idea – dealing with practical ('hard') issues – dealing with 'soft' issues – dealing with impact and wide-scale organisational issues. These can now be examined in more detail.

Stage 1 – Adoption of the idea

This is the stage when managers realise that use of the latest technology can improve the profit or the service level of the organisation, and the realisation that the cost of hardware, software and training must in the end be worth the overall output of the organisation and how the organisation is viewed. Worries about competitors – whatever the driving forces are – will push the managers to take decisions to invest heavily in cutting edge technology.

Stage 2 – Dealing with practical ('hard') issues

This is the difficult stage of choosing systems: selecting software and key personnel. Troublesome issues can arise, such as security problems, speed of access, legal matters, and worries about fraud and user authentication. However, although these problems may be problematic, they can be perceived as ESPs (easily solvable problems). This is because they are all solid, definable problems, which can be solved through strategic thinking or the creation of new policies to circumvent the difficulties.

Stage 3 – Dealing with 'soft' issues

This is the most difficult of all the stages – the time when some staff are beginning to accept the technology and work with it, and conversely the time when other staff present problems. This stage is likely to take up a considerable amount of the manager's time. Issues regarding trust; risk of losing old familiar systems; gaining new customers in new ways; training, retraining and redeployment are all inherent in this phase. These problems can be classified as DTCPs (difficult, time-consuming problems).

Stage 4 – Dealing with organisational issues

Wide-scale implementation of technology requires adjustment not just by the staff, employees, suppliers and customers but also by the fabric of the organisation itself. The technology is likely to change functions – it will create new jobs and erase established jobs.

This final stage is vital if e-commerce is to be accepted as a normal way of doing business. Many organisations get to this stage, but not through it. They linger somewhere in the twilight of not daring to make to make the final changes. The problems here are most difficult of all – and can involve a complete change of organisational culture, a notoriously difficult area to change. There is a lack of widely accepted and proven business models to push the organisation through this stage. However, as technology progresses, the number of models available in the marketplace will increase, which will assist organisations with this final stage.

Adoption of the idea
(managers become aware of the business
applications of latest technologies)
↓
Dealing with 'hard' issues
(easily solvable problems)
↓
Dealing with 'soft' issues
(difficult, time-consuming problems)
↓
Dealing with organisational issues
(the ongoing impact of changes)

Figure 1: The life cycle of the implementation of technology and exploitation of e-commerce in an organisation

Technology and leadership

Who leads the technological development in an organisation? The computing department? The administration department? The systems department? This is not an easy question to answer. Ultimately technology is there as a tool to be used to improve the organisation and while power may be delegated leadership is not. The ultimate leader must therefore always be the manager of the organisation. It is possible that the manager does not have the detailed knowledge held by the computing staff – nevertheless it is managers who are responsible for profit and loss and for improvement or worsening of services. This is especially the case in very large organisations, such as the National Health Service. Difficulties arise where an industry has become fragmented, such as the UK rail industry, which is now separated into companies responsible for different parts of the railway system. But in fragmented industries it is in many ways even more important to ensure there is sufficient leadership to be able to exploit the correct types of technology to their fullest extent. Peppard and Ward suggested that 'the relationship between the IT department and the rest of an organisation has been far from harmonious. The reason for this gap was found to be a cultural problem combined with the changing role of IT.'[5] It is thus essential to have leaders who can identify problems and adjust responsibilities.

Peppard and Ward also reported that some managers are disappointed with the benefits and value they are getting from the money invested in IT.[6] As a result, some organisations have decided to contract out IT requirements to a third party. This has led to a gap between the IT and the rest of the business. Other writers such as Allee have asked questions about whether IT resources are wasted in organisations as they are not fully understood or used by organisational members. Allee suggests that the 'interface between IT and the organisation is often misunderstood. If we don't understand what knowledge is, or how an organisation builds knowledge then it is very difficult to manage and support it with technology.'[7]

The whole issue of technology, leadership and the true exploitation of technology is one of the most difficult areas of management. There are many different perspectives, which all require special skills. These are looked at in the next section.

Skills required for managing the relationship between business and technology

The relationship between technology and business is one of the most complex to manage. We saw in chapter 2 how IT is no longer even an appropriate label – ICT is more accurate – to describe how we use technology in business communication. Some of the skills needed to drive ICT forward in terms of business success are:

- skills of flexibility – the ability to be flexible and open-minded

- clarity of thought – the ability to see clearly through all the tangles to what it is that the business wants to achieve, and then consider how technology can help

- bravery – having the courage not to be driven by the technology

- appreciation of team member's efforts and talents – the realisation that it is people not technology that make a business a success

- leadership skills – the realisation that steady leadership and not the control of the technology will drive forward the organisation.

Customers, organisational members, all those employed in the business chain, stakeholders of the organisation, the industry as a whole and the government all play a role in developing the relationship between technology and business. In order for that relationship to flourish clear communication and use of the above skills are essential.

References

1. Tomkins, R. 'A virtual investment', *Financial Times*, 17 December 2000, p. 26

2. DTI. *Clicks and Mortar: the New Store Fronts*. The retail e-commerce task force, commissioned by Retail and Consumer Services Foresight Panel and prepared by the ESRC Centre for Research on Innovation and Competition. London: DTI, 2000

3. Allcock, S. et al. *Business Information and the Internet*. London: The British Library. (British Library Research and Innovation Report 136.) Section 4: Barriers to the use of the internet, pp. 90–92

4. Commerce Net. 2000, *www.commercenet.com/Barriers2000study*

5. Peppard, J. and Ward, J. 'Reconciling the IT business relationship – a troubled marriage in need of guidance', *Journal of Strategic Information Systems* 5(1), March 1996, pp. 37–65

6. Peppard, J. and Ward, J. 'Mind the gap – diagnosing the relationship between the IT organisation and the rest of the business', *Journal of Strategic Management* 8(1), April 1999, pp. 29–60

7. Allee, V. *The Knowledge Evolution: Expanding Organisational Intelligence*. Boston: Butterworth-Heinemann, 1997

Web sites

Foresight – *www.foresight.gov.uk*

Chapter 4

Business strategy

Introduction

Planning and implementing a strategy has always been an important part of running a business. Strategic management and business strategy are phrases that indicate a fairly well-established plan within an organisation. The plan is normally created by following a pattern of ordered strategic thinking as follows.

- *Strategic analysis* The initial analysis of the organisation and the stage at which decisions are made regarding what the future goals are likely to be. Questions should be asked about the history of the organisation, such as: How did the organisation position itself in the past to be where it is today? Thought must be also be given to which external influences have affected the organisation in order that a clear picture can be built of the development of the organisation, which will assist with the creation of appropriate strategies in the future.

- *Strategic formulation* This includes the initial discussions regarding which strategies best fit the future plans of the organisation.

- *Strategic options* This phrase is linked to strategic formulation and is the stage where members of the organisation choose which theories can help the organisation in a real and practical way to achieve its goals.

- *Strategic implementation* This is concerned with how the chosen strategies are communicated, accepted and owned by individual members of an organisation. This is an essential stage on which can rest the success or failure of the entire strategic process.

- *Strategic evaluation* Questions need to be asked about how successful the process and the chosen strategy have been. This is also the stage for reflection and readjustment. If external environmental factors have changed dramatically then this is the time to realise the next strategy, to ensure it always fits the goals of the organisation.

The aim of this chapter is to give a brief overview of some of the main issues in strategic management within the above framework but from the following perspectives: analysis of the organisation, categorisation of strategy, the importance of strategic options and strategic fit, examination of the environment at strategic level, controlling strategy, the place of knowledge management and the evaluation of strategic options. The chapter closes by looking at the skills required of an effective strategic manager.

Strategic analysis of the organisation

In order to understand strategy, we first need to take a step back and carefully consider various aspects of the organisation. The most fundamental consideration involves thinking about the reason why any particular organisation exists in the first place – what are the prime functions of the organisation? It has been said that organisations have to carry out four functions to be successful.[1] These have been defined as the performance of goal-orientated tasks, management of the environment, the task of encouraging people in the organisation to work together and establishing common ways of dealing with outsiders. All these areas need careful thought concerning how a new strategy would impact on each function in order for the organisation to survive.

Another reason for close examination of this kind is that once an organisation has been analysed using a particular model it enables the strategist to work through each part of the organisation to consider how the various strategies will provide the best fit to help the organisation achieve its goals. If models are not used in the planning of strategy there is a danger that the process may become based on vague ideas that lack focus and become very difficult to implement successfully.

There are many models of organisations but one of the best known and easiest to use for our purposes is that created by Mintzberg.[2] Mintzberg identified five basic parts of an organisation:

- the operating core – members of the organisation who carry out the day-to-day work of the company

- the strategic apex – the power held by a few managers near the top of a pyramid structure

- the middle line – middle managers who report to the strategic apex

- the technostructure – members of the organisation who are responsible for seeing to the needs of the organisation such as computing departments

- support staff – those who work outside the main product area but provide essential support roles.

This model of the five-part organisation is normally surrounded by a further sixth idea – that of 'ideology'. Mintzberg's work in this area identified the fact that all parts of the organisation are affected by the organisation's underlying ethics and that this in turn will affect the nature and culture of the organisation.

Mintzberg also proposed that organisations could be categorised by type, depending on their characteristics. He argued that a certain type of strategy was likely to be found within each one of these categories.

- *In entrepreneurial organisations* staff are encouraged to try out new ideas. Here the strategy is likely to be visionary, very flexible and quickly able to respond to changes.

- *In machine organisations,* which are likely to be well ordered and formal, the strategy is likely to be planned, characterised by strong control but paying little heed to people issues.

- *In professional organisations,* where the strategy is likely to be fragmented and contain lots of detail, the organisation will be democratic but difficult to control and co-ordinate.

- *In diversified organisations* strategy is likely to be fairly rigid with policy issued by corporate headquarters.

- *In innovative organisations*, likely to be full of creativity yet difficult to control, the ideology is likely to be that of learning by doing.

- *In missionary organisations* – charities and voluntary organisations – the strategy is likely to be very central to the organisation. The structure is likely to be that of small operating units based on a strong ideology, which is shared by most members of the organisation.

Mintzberg's classification of the parts of the organisation can be used as a checklist when deciding on strategies as we have an idea of types of organisations and the kinds of strategies that seem to have been prevalent and successful in the past. However, it is important to remember that organisations change as society develops in different directions and to use models as flexible frameworks to assist with the strategic process and not as a rigid guide to strategic management.

There is an important distinction between deliberate and emergent strategies. A deliberate strategy is one that is deliberate, planned and seen through to completion. An emergent strategy can be defined as one that almost happens by accident or evolves naturally without much prior planning or thought. Both kinds of strategy are seen as perfectly acceptable and in many organisations both types of strategy may happen simultaneously – but often only the formal one is recognised.

Finally, strategy is affected by the way in which decisions are made in the organisation. According to Cooke and Slack the decision-making process in the organisation must take into account two separate but linked needs.[3] These are that when problems first arise it is important to ensure that decisions are actually taken and to be confident that these decisions are the right ones and good for the organisation. We could add to this that decisions need to be taken by the appropriate people, that decisions need to be evaluated and that decisions should be guided by the overall strategy of the organisation. Whatever strategy is chosen it must be designed to encourage all aspects of the decision-making process.

The importance of closely examining the organisation before creating strategy is therefore of paramount importance. Setting up frameworks by using models to check each aspect of the organisation is a vital tool, which can be used to ensure the success of the strategic management of the organisation.

The categorisation and formulation of strategy

Haberberg and Rieple have identified different categories of strategy,[4] based on newer ideas as well as classical schools of thought:

- visionary strategy – created by the vision of a single leader

- planning strategy – undertaken as a meticulous and carefully orchestrated process

- decision preference strategy – based on individual thought processes

- process strategy – based on the organisation's history

- political strategy – based on negotiation and power centres

- ecological strategy – where the organisation tries to adapt to the changes in the physical environment (the external environment)

- organisational anarchy – where an organisation lacks any kind of obvious strategy.

The job of the strategist is to identify which one of these strategies best suits the organisation and the people in it, and then to implement the strategy successfully throughout the organisation. This sounds very straightforward in terms of the theory of strategy making but the reality is that organisations are very messy to deal with and clear-cut situations are seldom found. New areas of strategy need to be developed in order to fulfil today's new work patterns of short-lived tasks, short-term contract work, flexible work methods and short-term project teams. How do these areas fit into established areas of strategy? Some suggestions for new ways of viewing strategy, which may fit the new patterns, are discussed below.

- *Strategy needs to be fluid* Strategy need not be consistent across the organisation but may be altered for different areas of the organisation. This is a radical rethink of earlier theories.

- *Strategies can be short lived* This is another break with established thinking. Long-term, short-term and medium-term strategies then become single, short project strategies, which are triangulated in the organisation by linking the organisation's prime goal with a relevant departmental objective and the objective of the project. Once this task is achieved the group and the associated strategy are disbanded.

In order for these ideas to work the overarching strategy of the organisation must be flexible enough to allow individual teams to make and implement their own decisions, yet provide clear focus for the organisation to achieve its goals. However, there will always need to be a close fit of the organisation's overall goals with the chosen strategies and this is discussed in the next section.

Strategic options and strategic fit

Strategic fit is about selecting a strategy that best fits the organisation, taking all of the above issues into account. Strategies can be said to have a tight fit or a loose fit – most often they are not static but change over time. In management terms this changing process is know as the life cycle of ideas, which ranges from development through to growth, into maturity and finally into decline.

To achieve strategic fit, organisation members must reach agreement on the goals of the organisation while considering the culture of the organisation and the risk factor of implementing a particular strategy. Can the strategy be characterised as high or low risk? Is it, for example, high risk short term or low risk short term – decisions must be made about whatever combination is appropriate. Thought must also be given to how these issues are viewed by management, stakeholders, competitors and members of the organisation.

Examination of the environment at a strategic level

We have already discussed the importance of clearly identifying an organisation's external environment. There is also a way of examining the environment at a strategic level by using Porter's 'five forces analysis' model.[5] These are the forces that affect the level of competition in industry and are designed to assist the strategist to identify the basis of competition or to decide on where within that competition they should best place themselves. Porter's five forces are described below.

The threat of entry This depends on the threat to which there are barriers to entry of a particular industry for a new or established company. These are normally:

- economies of scale
- capital cost of entry (to a new industry)
- access to distribution channels
- cost advantages such as discounts
- expected retaliation by other companies already present in the industry
- legislation or government regulations
- differentiation of the product.

The key is to find out which barriers exist, explore all available options, identify which is the most lethal and which is the weakest and then make decisions about which strategy can be used to the organisation's advantage in order to gain competitive edge.

Power of buyers and *power of suppliers* The second and third force in Porter's model are the power status of the buyers and suppliers, which are linked together as these forces are inextricably related. Buyer power is high if there are a few buyers that dominate the market and supplier power is said to be high if there are a few suppliers who are able to set whatever price structure they believe the market will withstand.

Threat of substitute products The fourth aspect of the model is the threat of substitute products – the threat that another company could manufacture a product that is very similar to the product in question, but is differentiated in some way, for instance by price or quality.

Competitive rivalry The fifth barrier to entry is the one that acts as the centre of all the other forces – competitive rivalry. All the forces mentioned need to be in balance and to the advantage of the company. The important strategic issue surrounding Porter's model is the decision about what competitive position is best for the organisation and helps to maintain competitive advantage. Related to this is the issue of strategic thinking. In 2001 Bonn found that 'lack of thinking by managers seemed to be a major problem'.[6] His study suggested that strategic thinking needs to be addressed at two levels – individual and strategic. The research concluded that by successfully integrating theses two levels a critical 'core competency' will be created, which, used in conjunction with Porter's model, can then form the basis of a solid competitive advantage.

Controlling strategy

There is a variety of theories that discuss the best ways of controlling strategy. Strategy needs to be controlled in order to prevent or correct the following problems: that the strategy has not been adequately planned out, that there are too many risks associated with a particular strategy that have not been taken into account, that the strategy is too rigid and not fluid enough to respond quickly to a changing environment and goal conflict where the goals of the strategy do not match the goals of the organisation. One model[7] analysed strategic control as having four key variables:

- core values and conflict of core values
- risks to be avoided
- strategic uncertainty
- critical performance variables of the various functions of the organisation.

Each one of these variables can be used as a checklist at different times throughout the life of the strategy to ensure it is still appropriate to the organisation's needs.

The place of knowledge management

Knowledge management can be defined as the way in which an organisation collects and organises all its information needs. It is the bringing together of external and internal information in such a way that it makes the organisation more effective and efficient. It the basis of what makes the organisation a capable and successful business. In general, there are two 'classical' categories of knowledge – tacit knowledge and explicit knowledge. The first of these, tacit knowledge, can be defined as knowledge which is derived from logic or common sense. It is knowledge that we inherently 'know' to be right. Explicit knowledge is knowledge gained from learning specific information for instance by reading or academic accomplishment. Whether knowledge management is seen as a strategy on its own merit or as part of the overall strategy of the organisation is still open to debate. However, within the organisation there are considerations that will affect the way in which knowledge management is approached regarding the formality of the organisation, the size, age and the industry in which the organisation operates.

How does the formality of the organisation affect the way in which the organisation operates with regard to knowledge management? Most studies have shown that large bureaucratic organisations tend to be formal and rigid, but are usually very effective at achieving goals and providing a quality service or product. More flexible organisations may have a more relaxed culture and still produce quality output, while being pleasanter places to work for members of the organisation, thus enhancing the motivation of people. Knowledge management is likely to be approached in different ways by both types of organisation – by building it into an existing structure in the formal organisation and by creating a structure around a concept in the informal organisation.

The age of the organisation is another important factor. Younger organisations tend to be smaller and more technology-orientated and therefore more open and immediately suited to a knowledge management type of environment. However, many older, established organisations tend to be in the process of structural and usually cultural change and are therefore very receptive to new ideas and strategies and easily able to incorporate knowledge management into their overall strategy.

The size of the organisation is also significant. The old axiom has always been that larger organisations are difficult and messy to manage. However, many organisations are aware of the need to change and are adapting to flexible methods of working and using new information and communications technology and implementing new work patterns for short-life project teams. Some organisations are almost beginning to operate like individuals pods, which are managed from within, have a short existence and then disperse. In this case effective knowledge management is essential.

Profit organisations such as manufacturing are seen as fairly straightforward organisations where the ultimate goal – profit – is clear to all members of the organisation. Knowledge management goals would normally be in line with the goal of the organisation, thereby creating what is known as goal congruence.

Public sector organisations such as government organisations and most educational establishments are also beginning to benefit from the introduction of knowledge management. The goal of these organisations is usually service-oriented but is further complicated by the fact that there are so many interested and active stakeholders who sometimes have conflicting goals. Effective knowledge management in these organisations is much more difficult due to the spread of diverse interests and goals.

Charitable or voluntary organisations whose goal is usually to raise funds or to give practical assistance are also beginning to be aware of the benefits of knowledge management. In these organisations knowledge management may be badly needed but the goals are such that the time and money required to be invested in this area is not available in the smaller organisation of this type. However, the larger, more established, charities are aware of this issue and some now employ knowledge management workers. The goals of these charities are clear and are usually owned by all members of the organisation.

Knowledge management is increasingly accepted as an important strategy by all types of organisation and it is an important factor when considering strategic options. It is an area that is constantly changing and for which a British Standard will shortly be available. A report produced PricewaterhouseCoopers for the BSI may be useful for those considering implementing knowledge management in an organisation.[8]

Evaluation of strategic options

Haberberg and Rieple have developed the following ideas for the evaluation of strategic options within an organisation's strategic plan.[9]

- The resources to implement the option need to be readily available.

- The option must be acceptable to all the stakeholders who operate within the external and internal environment.

- The option must be consistent with other existing plans.

- The option needs to be effective – it needs to be an actual solution to the problem.

- The option must be sustainable – the option must contribute to some element of individuality to the organisation's competitive edge.

Strategic evaluation is important and needs to be balanced and objective. The key is to keep the evaluation simple by using a checklist that can easily be followed by all members of the organisation.

The skills required of an effective strategic manager

Effective communication has always been the keystone of good management and within business strategy this is as important as ever. The slow acceptability of short-term strategies, such as six to ten weeks for the duration of a project, will make good communication increasingly important. The management of this kind of a strategy requires new skills in order to adjust issues and to relate short-term plans to the overall goals of the organisation. The kinds of strategic control that are to be put in place for these new ideas to work need to be quite different from those that we have become accustomed to in the past.

The main skills and attributes required for an efficient and effective strategist are clarity of mind, an ability to be objective, an ability to think creatively, an ability to think across levels, and an ability to connect previously unrelated issues in order to pick up possible future trends. The analysis of the internal and external environment, clear decision-making about where the organisation is at any one moment and where it needs to be positioned in the future are all essential elements in the building and evaluating of strategy. It is no longer enough just to evaluate options and choose what seems to be the correct one – in the competitive world it is vital that the issue of the future existence of the organisation is always considered. These skills will be needed by someone carrying out what might be a new role in the organisation – that of strategic option controller. This role was perhaps previously undertaken by a senior manager who dealt with complex issues in the organisation but was unable, due to resources or the structure and outlook of the organisation, to focus clearly on strategic issues.

It is also important that strategic managers are able to use and exploit knowledge management in line with the type of organisation in which they work. The authority given to knowledge management analysts in some organisations is such that they are able to take into account factors such as the age, size and the type of industry that would be involved before embarking on new projects – and are able to take an active and important part in the creation and implementation of strategy. This role was formerly carried out by a variety of personnel, such as information officers or IT specialists. It will take time before the role of the knowledge management analyst is clear.

If these two new roles of strategic option controller and knowledge management analyst are allowed to develop in organisations together they will provide a new way of analysing information and comparing strategic options, which has not been possible in the past. These key roles will enable strategic management to move forward and deal with new issues in a progressive and exciting way, to ensure the success of all organisations.

References

1. Mintzberg, H. *The Structuring of Organisations: a Synthesis of the Research*. New York: Prentice Hall, 1979

2. Mintzberg, H. *Mintzberg on Management*. New York: Free Press, 1989

3. Cooke, S and Slack, N. *Making Management Decisions*. NewYork: Prentice Hall, 1984

4. Haberberg, A. and Rieple, A. *The Strategic Management of Organisations*. Harlow: Financial Times/ Prentice Hall, 2001

5. Porter, M.E. *Competitive Strategy: Techniques for Analysing Industries and Competitors*. New York: Free Press, 1980

6. Bonn, I. 'Developing strategic thinking as a core competency', *Management Decision* 63(1), 2001, pp. 63–71

7. Simons, R. *Levers of Control* Boston: Harvard Business School, 1995

8. Kelleher, D. and Levine, S. *PAS 2001 – Knowledge Management: a Guide to Good Practice*. Prepared by PricewaterhouseCoopers on behalf of BSI. London: BSI, 2001

9. Haberberg, A. and Rieple, A. *The Strategic Management of Organisations*. Harlow: Financial Times/ Prentice Hall, 2001

The Phenomenal Power of Business Intelligence

Chapter 5

The changing nature of marketing

Introduction

The marketing of an organisation is one of the crucial functions of management. The way a product or service is presented to the relevant industry and to society as a whole forms the basis of opinion concerning how an organisation is perceived. This chapter is about marketing the organisation but questions whether the nature of marketing is changing due to the growth of knowledge management. Organisations are increasingly using information in terms of knowledge investments and knowledge and it is possible that most marketing functions will eventually be subsumed under the heading of knowledge management. If this is so then there is also an issue surrounding the expansion of the role of the knowledge manager. This role may be in danger of growing to such an extent that the organisation needs to set clear boundaries or the job of the knowledge manager will become unmanageable.

There are four prime sections of marketing, known collectively as the marketing mix: product, promotion, price and place. These need to be carefully balanced in order to create the correct environment for a marketing plan to be successful. All four principles need to work in harmony with each other based on effective market research, which will result in an effective and successful marketing plan. This chapter is not intended to be a step-by-step guide of how to market an organisation as there are a plethora of detailed textbooks on marketing, such as the one by Kotler.[1] Instead, the chapter provides information on the basic principles of marketing through explanations of market research and each of the four concepts of the marketing mix. In addition, there are discussions about the knowledge manager's role within each function. The chapter closes with a summary of new skills pertinent to the changing nature of marketing.

Market research

Market research can be defined as the collection and collation of information, which allows sound decisions to be made concerning the manufacture and sale of a product or a service. Market research can take many forms, from random samples of public opinion to very specific targeting of narrowly defined groups of people. These groups are classified using a method known as market segmentation, which concerns the analysis of the market using different criteria. For example, the market can be defined in terms of demographics – age, race, lifestyle, gender – and by regional, national, European or international forms of geographical location. There are a myriad of combinations of criteria with which markets can be identified. The success of the marketing mix depends to a great extent on selling the right product to the right market.

The information collected through the market research process is collated, analysed and used in the organisation to make decisions concerning some kind of marketing plan. This assumes that the organisation has effective information systems, which allow the correct information to be fed to various levels of the organisation. If knowledge management can be defined as being about how an organisation uses its information assets, then is market research, which is based on information, really about the way in which knowledge is used and stored in the organisation? Is there a possibility that what used to be known as market research is now in danger of being subsumed under the heading of knowledge management? If we choose to agree to this assertion and follow a logical line of reasoning then the entire marketing mix perhaps needs to be relabelled as a 'knowledge asset marketing mix'. This would demonstrate the need for a different view of the way in which information is perceived in the organisation – both by members of the organisation and by the general public. However, one could argue that changing the name of a marketing model and relabelling roles in an organisation does not necessarily change their functions. Functions in organisations are not as rigid and inflexible as they once were, and if the management style is one that is open to change then perhaps there will be not only some renaming of functions but also some radical changes in roles in future.

Product

The product can be analysed using a four-dimensional framework:

- market penetration – selling an established product to an established market

- market extension – selling an established product to new market
- product development – selling a new product to an already well-established market
- diversification – selling a new product to a new market.

This model is a classical framework based on work undertaken by Ansoff.[2] Each of these strategies contains an element of risk, from the least risky (selling an established product to an established market) to the most risky (selling a new product to a new market). A good example of a diversified company is Virgin, which sells travel, pensions and music recordings – different products – to different sections of markets. This is not to say that there is no overlap between these markets but that the markets for the total products are able to expand fully and take into account different sections of the community.

Within a company the sales of a particular product will change over a period of time. This change in sales patterns is known in marketing terms as the product's life cycle.

There are five clear stages in the sale of a product. These are:

- the introduction of a product to the market
- the growth of sales as the product becomes familiar to consumers
- maturity of the product as demand is more or less fully met
- saturation of the market (when all the consumers who want the product have already purchased it)

- decline of the sales of the product when it is no longer popular or is taken over by the benefits provided by new or different products or services.

Each of these stages happens over a period of time so that demand is slow at first but builds up, reaching the highest point of demand at the saturation stage. This is usually the point when price wars start in order to compete for the very best sales. This is because the saturation stage precedes the final stage of decline. In order to compensate for the decline stage companies plan constantly to introduce new products so that there are always several products in the early stages of the life cycle in order to maintain maximum profits. This is known as the product portfolio. New products are then introduced consecutively, which is known as product succession.

Many decisions need to be made when considering what strategies the company will use to plan out its product portfolio. One of the most widely used models to assist with these kind of decisions is the one created by the Boston Consulting Group. This is a four-point matrix, which employs certain terms to describe how a product is perceived in relation to the profit it will generate for the company. The terms are:

- *stars* – products fairly new in the market, well liked by the consumer and hence achieving a high market share in an expanding market

- *cash cows* – products that are stable; they already have high market share but the market for the product is not expanding; likely to be thoroughly tested and aimed at a specific market segment

- *problem children* – very new products, which are still in the early stage of development; likely in future years – if all goes well – to move towards the *star* category; have low market share but there is potential for a reasonable size of the market in the future

- *dogs* – products that no longer generate profit; they have a low market share and are stagnant.

Using this framework a classical strategy would be to use the cash generated by the *cash cow* products to create new *stars* and to develop some of the *problem children*. However, in order to follow this strategy through and to make decisions good quality information is needed. Without an efficient and effective information flow the model could not be used, strategy could not be created, and there would be limited new product development and low profit sales. The role of the knowledge manager is essential in order to exploit the investment in information that organisations make in terms of product development.

Promotion

The key to the promotion of the product is not the product in itself but the perceived need of the benefits of the product. For example, some mobile phone companies now offer mobiles that are known as a communicators and can instantly provide access to the Internet – here speed is the key benefit that would be used to promote the product. The second key to the success of promotion is consistent communication. This means that at all times the product must be discussed in a particular way that extols its virtues. All members of the sales teams and members of the organisation must carry a similar message so that the organisation's view of the product is translated into the consciousness of the consumer. Choosing how to promote a product is an important decision, which should be linked to the strategy of the organisation. In general there are four ways of promoting a product: personal selling, advertising, sales promotion and Internet selling. Each one of the four groups has advantages and disadvantages as discussed below.

Personal selling is just that – personal – and involves person-to-person contact. This means that sales staff are knowledgeable about customers and can explain details of highly technical products directly to the consumer. The disadvantage of personal selling is that it can be expensive in terms of staff time but this can be offset against the profits gained.

Advertising can take many forms, such as advertising through media format – television, newspapers and magazines. Advertising is said to have three main purposes: to inform the consumer about new products, to persuade the public of the benefits of the products and to reinforce existing views that a purchase was a good choice and matches a certain lifestyle. There are two distinct types of advertising – one is business-to-business advertising and the second is business-to-consumer advertising. Both groups use the communication channels of the Internet to advertise their products. For example, the bookseller Amazon dot.com, which sells books directly to the public at reasonable rates, has been very successful – it has also been successful at advertising its name on other sites on the Internet. However, in 2002 the company was at the stage when competition for similar products was high. There is also direct mail advertising, which is useful in raising awareness of products or information concerning sales events. On the whole the success of direct mail advertising depends on an accurate mailing list in order to ensure that the right product is being marketed to the appropriate customer.

Sales promotions concerning new or discounted stock are available in many forms – from discount vouchers to special offers and competitions where the aim is to move stock earlier and faster.

Internet selling is effective but is selling to a defined market in terms of computer access. However, most members of the public do now have access to Internet facilities either at home, at work, in Internet cafés or through public libraries. Internet selling has advantages – it allows customers to search for the best price and have goods delivered to the door. The disadvantage is that it involves no sales talk and thus no opportunity to 'sell' the products to the customers. Future trends in this area are likely to include an increase in the use of tailored messages delivered to specific customers as the number of consumers who have Internet links increases.

The implications of promotion to the role of the knowledge manager is likely to be in terms of the importance of consistency of communication. Control of communication and communication channels are vital to the success of the promotion strategy. The role of the knowledge manager is likely to become more closely defined as one that deals with tacit as well as explicit knowledge and can provide valuable assistance in managing the marketing of the organisation.

Price

The price of a product is based on two factors: how much the item cost to manufacture and the price the market will stand. These factors are linked to all the other aspects of the marketing mix.

Pricing strategies are always risky as if a product is priced too high it will cease to be in demand, yet the price must be high enough to be in balance with the image of the product, whether at the luxury or the discounted end of the market. The product must be priced correctly so as to meet the correct level of repeat purchase. For instance, cars may be purchased no more than once every few years whereas other items such as food and toiletries are fast repeat items. Fast repeat items are generally priced lower than slow repeat items as profit is made from the volume and bulk of the purchased items.

The pricing decision is influenced by a model known as the 'demand curve', where if the price is too high demand drops, the product is not sold, the organisation loses money and the competition is able to undercut the price. The opposing scenario is that, if the price is set too low, demand for the product may be high but the product may be easily copied therefore increasing competition for the product. There are other factors in this equation, such as the quality of the product, the image of the product, whether the product is seasonal and where the product is sold. In general there is usually what is known as a 'trade off point', where costs are covered and the price is at a level where demand is reasonably satisfactory. Other factors that affect the pricing decision are the price of overheads (including salaries), whether any special skills are needed and whether new members of the organisation can be trained quickly. It may be that the degree of skills required are such that all training must be complete and thoroughly tested before the product or service can be fully operational and offered to the public.

It is difficult to define a clear role for the knowledge manager in the area of pricing issues. However, the established role of the knowledge manager as the controller and gatekeeper of information is a very important one in providing access to the necessary information. It is crucial to the success of the organisation that the knowledge manager is able to oversee the flexible flow of information in order to allow correct pricing decisions to be taken.

Place

The place where goods are sold is vital in adding – or taking away from – the perceived quality or image of the goods. The ambience of the location where goods are bought is almost as important as the goods themselves. In addition, the way in which they are presented and packaged is essential in maintaining the desired image of the product.

Within the distribution process there are six recognised key decision areas:

- major strategic decisions – those decisions that concern the size and number of warehouses, levels of service, and the location of new stores

- stock decisions – the cost of holding stock and decisions about methods of stock control

- communications decisions – which can only be made if the relevant, current information is available in an appropriate format; this depends in turn on the way in which information flows within the organisation

- delivery decisions – taking into account other factors such as costs of containers

- transport decisions – concerning consideration of cost

- production decisions – for example, how many items to manufacture to meet estimated demand.

The forecasting of demand for each product is an important element in the success of the marketing mix. The need for good quality market research information, which is linked to obvious or hidden trends, is essential.

Another aspect of this part of the marketing mix is the way in which goods actually reach the consumer. There are several classical distribution channels, namely manufacturer to customer, manufacturer to retailer to customer, and manufacturer to wholesaler to retailer. There is sometimes also a much longer chain, which would involve the chain of manufacturer to agent, to wholesaler, to retailer, and finally to customer.

The rise in the popularity of call centres and Internet shopping has added another channel of distribution. Some call centres sell direct – a quick method of selling, which usually has low costs for the producer and is an accepted method of selling in 2003. As we discussed earlier, Internet shopping is also increasing in popularity. Indeed, the impact of technology on marketing has been such that marketing trends are changing. For example, Relationship Marketing, which is concerned with developing one-to-one relationships over a number of years, is becoming more popular as the Internet allows the maintenance of very close, customised relationships with many, rather than a few, customers.

How can decisions be made about which channel to choose? This depends on many factors, including where the customer will expect to see the product, what level of support the product requires and how fast the product will take to sell.

These basic principles have one factor in common – they require information that is accurate, up to date and that can be easily distributed to the correct parts of the organisation. This is the start of knowledge management. As we have seen, knowledge management is fundamentally about the collation of external and internal information to ensure the maximum success of the organisation.

Skills pertinent to the changing nature of marketing

This chapter began with a radical assertion – that the role of a knowledge manager is expanding to such an extent that those undertaking this role may be able to function as part of the organisation's marketing team. This is in the terms of information provision for market research and the management of information that takes place during the process of marketing a product. Organisations are perhaps moving towards a new model of working practice but in reality the beginning of the 21st century is one of transition. Platts and Yeung stated that 'knowledge management has emerged as a critical issue for organisations and their management to address. It is argued that one reason why there is discontent with current approaches is because too much emphasis has been placed on explicit knowledge, with the neglect of tacit knowledge.'[3] Establishing knowledge management within an organisation creates an equal forum for both types of information to be combined. It is essential that business organisations need to be ready for the unexpected and to be able to react quickly to sudden events, such as the deliberate destruction of the World Trade Center in New York on 11 September 2001, which led to global repercussions in the stock markets. The huge knowledge assets of, for example, the insurance and investment companies contained in the World Trade Center did not disappear when the building collapsed as the tacit knowledge was embedded in the organisation and available through other branches in locations throughout the world.

The key skills and pieces of knowledge that are needed to be a knowledge manager include technology skills, knowledge of the organisation's structure, knowledge of organisational roles, information retrieval skills, information collation skills and the ability to be objective and alert to new ideas in the literature. All of these are skills also used in marketing roles. Martin identifies the links between knowledge management and business benefits as being about three factors: customer intimacy, operational excellence and achieving product leadership.[4] Each of these areas is information-based and requires the skills of a knowledge manager who is able to apply external knowledge and encourage the sharing of internal knowledge in order to enhance the marketing function.

It has been argued that the success of future business organisations will be based on the ability to continually create new products and services[5] and that this can only be achieved by continual innovation.[6] The key to good innovation is to employ the technique of collaborative-based knowledge management by loosening the former rigid functions in organisations and encouraging the sharing and overlapping of roles, and even on occasion the merging of roles for short periods. By allowing knowledge managers to collaborate with the marketing functions of an organisation in this way this new combination of roles will create a new type of flexible organisation.

Marketing continues to be an essential element in catering to the ever-changing tastes of the discerning consumer. In order to enhance this function it is vital to encourage the new role of knowledge managers to develop alongside established marketing roles. This will call for clear vision, brave and courageous thinking and for organisational commitment to a shift towards a new model of working. By bringing together the two aspects of information – knowledge management and marketing – and by adjusting strategies and linking information flows we are witnessing the creation of new organisational patterns and practices of the 21st century.

References

1. Kotler, P. *Marketing Management: Analysis, Planning, Marketing and Control*, 9th int. ed. New Jersey: Prentice Hall, 2001

2. Ansoff, H.I. *Corporate Strategy*. London: Penguin, 1977

3. Platts, M.J. and Yeung M.B. 'Managing learning and tacit knowledge', *Strategic Change* 9(6), Sept–Oct 2000, pp. 347–55.

4. Martin, W.J. 'The role of knowledge content in e-commerce', *Journal of Information Science* 27(3), 2001, pp. 180–4

5. Miles, R.E. et al. 'The future dot org', *Long Range Planning* 33(3), June 2000, pp. 300–21

Chapter 6

Managing organisational relationships

Introduction

The majority of management textbooks include a chapter 'Managing the human resource'. The aim of these chapters is generally to find ways of motivating staff to take actions that will help the organisation achieve its goal. Traditional theories on motivation (many of which were established during the Industrial Revolution) are still to be found within the curriculum of most management-orientated degrees. These theories deal with motivation, in the classic context of managing staff who work on site within an organisation. However, as we are now in the 21st century, motivation needs to be considered within the context of new work patterns, such as teleworking, flexiworking and working from remote locations, and to deal with the concept of the paperless office. It has been suggested that there are certain policies that the manager should adopt in order to realise employees' potential within this new enviroment.[1] These include clear identification of any problems emerging in organisations as a result of new work trends, an emphasis on recognition of individual successes, transparent decision-making procedures, efficient verbal and electronic communication systems and properly managed, and effective, knowledge management systems. These are all vital issues and factors in motivating employees in a new context.

This chapter explores how organisational relationships can be better managed within the new context. There is a discussion of traditional views of the process of management and the role of the manager in relation to network structures and processes and alternative types of managing, such as creative management. The chapter closes with an analysis of methods of controlling the organisation, consideration of some international perspectives of managing organisations, and a brief discussion of the skills required to manage organisational relationships.

Traditional views of the process of management

In 1949 Fayol suggested that there were 14 main areas of a manager's work and identified these as the main functions of management in the mid-20th century.[2] They are:

- division of work
- authority
- responsibility
- discipline
- unity of command
- unity of direction
- subordination of individual interest to the general interest

- remuneration of personnel
- centralisation
- establishing a chain of authority
- order
- equity
- stability of tenure of personnel
- encouragement of initiative and the development of an 'esprit de corps' within the organisation.

How far do these processes translate into life for the manager today?

The division of work has now become the allocation of tasks in a flexible working environment. Authority and responsibility have become devolved as employees are increasingly empowered. A fundamental part of the manager's tasks is to deal with issues of discipline – areas of misconduct are usually clearly set out in a work contract. The unit of command is now often loose and flexible; unity of direction is now dependent on the goals of each small team or task. The encouragement of subordination of individual interest to the general interest is probably still true though hidden agendas will sometimes be present. The remuneration of personnel remains a fundamental cause of motivation and is still expected to be dealt with by senior managers. Centralisation systems and styles have changed over time to decentralisation and sometimes back to centralisation but the main change has been the flexibility to undertake these changes. The importance of keeping the chain of authority is still an element of a manager's task but this function tends not to be as rigid as it was in the past and many managers are willing to alter the organisation's structure to accommodate new ideas. The area of order – ensuring the smooth running of the organisation – is still seen as a vital part of management. Equity is now viewed as equal opportunities, and legislation in this area is strict and must be adhered to by all parties. Stability of tenure of personnel – generally stability of employment – has shifted to contract work and an increase in part-time work: one, two or even three different careers are now expected in a lifetime. As for initiative, innovation and creativity are encouraged in most forward-thinking organisations. Finally, management responsibility for esprit de corps – trust and a sense of shared ownership of all knowledge and expertise – are essential in order to provide true knowledge management for all members of the organisation.

So, we can see that in many respects original ideas from Fayol's work in 1949 have not radically altered but have become moulded into a modern day setting – many principles and ideas are still seen as valid. Do other traditional management ideas still have validity?

Burns and Stalker proposed organic and mechanistic theories of management.[3] The established terms may perhaps be translated into the following modern day equivalents. The mechanistic view of very precise definitions of rights and obligations can be translated into today's detailed contracts of work. However, this view does not really allow for any fluidity or flexibility in the management of the organisation. The alternative, organic view is more forward thinking as this emphasises the importance of networking, teamwork, commitment to technology and so on.

There are numerous traditional theories that involve classical, scientific and behavioural schools of management. All theories can have some bearing on modern day management techniques but what is important is that managers have choices in the way in which they manage. Vroom and Yetton identified five basic styles of management.[4]

- The manager makes decisions personally, using information that is immediately available.

- The manager obtains required information from subordinates and then make a decision. Involvement by others is limited to the provision of information.

- The manager discusses the problem with subordinates individually, while still retaining the decision-making role.

- The manager discusses the problem collectively with subordinates, encouraging collective thoughts and ideas, while still retaining the decision-making role.

- The problem is discussed and tackled as a group. The manager and subordinates attempt to reach a consensus on a solution, which is then adopted.

This work was undertaken in 1970s. What relevance does this have for the way in which we require and need managers to function in the present climate? Do managers manage in all these ways simultaneously? Can they still do this if the workers are remote? An answer to these and other questions can perhaps be answered by examining the second part of the authors' work. The research gave careful consideration to how managers make decisions and concluded that the decision-making process was based on the type of decision that needed to be made – on what they termed 'dimensions', identified as follows:

- the quality dimension – where there is a need for a high quality solution

- the information dimension – where the location of information and who needs to have access to the information is considered

- the commitment dimension – where there needs to be commitment to the outcome of the decision

- the capability dimension – where a group needs to be capable of making a practical, objective decision.

The information dimension is of particular importance in the management of remote workers and in the associated areas of knowledge management. It is likely that managers do not have one-dimensional thinking but will be thinking about problems and solutions from many different angles. All these dimensions are relevant today. Members of the organisation need to consider that they are involved in decisions and that their opinion and expertise are valued resources.

So, on the whole, management thinking has developed, moved forward and changed shape to fit different organisations. The next section will examine whether the shape of management – the role of the manager – now fits the new patterns of work.

The role of the manager in relation to network structures and processes

The role of the manager is normally about making decisions based on good quality information. However, many problems are complex and exist in a very fluid, fast-changing world. One writer asked: 'How can enormously complex problems, involving competing and interwoven social, cultural, ethical and personal issues, as well as economic ones, be integrated into coherent wholes?'[5] In order to answer this question we can look at management within another context – that of networking. Managing can also be seen as being about networking and exploiting the results of networking to gain competitive edge for an organisation. The nature of networking has changed considerably over the past 20 years. To examine these differences in more detail we can look at writers from this era and the way in which networking was then defined. The following five characteristics of network structures were identified in organisations in 1982.[6]

- The organisation was seen as self-reliant with autonomous participants. The structure was independent yet had interdependent parts.

- Networking took place on many levels as a result of networks interconnecting on an ever-expanding scale from local to national to international.

- Distributed powers and responsibility flowed along horizontal or wavy lines, not rigid vertical lines.

- The organisation was seen as having an 'all round perception', a single focus that included an ability to perceive in different ways.

- The structures were seen as having many leaders yet few rings of power, a kind of 'hydra-headed direction'.

The same writers also identified five characteristics of network processes.

- Professional relationships were abstract and qualitative as well as concrete and quantitative.

- 'Fuzziness', i.e. networks seemed to have a lack of clarity – there was a lack of inner divisions and the borderlines were indistinct.

- Nodes and links were important entry points for connectors conveying information.

- Equal importance was vital, according equal importance to the individual and the group.

- The value of information was also deemed to be important, as was the value of others – interdependence on others versus self-interest.

These features can be seen in today's organisation and the role of managers in the present day. The characteristics of network structures in the 21st century are listed below.

- There has been an increase in teamwork on short-term projects; sections tend to be fragmented yet are usually working towards common goals.

- There is a tendency for all networking to be international and global; this is now seen as the norm.

- Distribution of power is now seen as very transient as power fluctuates with working patterns.

- All round perception has changed since there has been an emphasis on the sharing of information rather than the hiding of information – perception is now more open.

- Power is now very devolved: the organisational structure ceases to be as important when people have a strong sense of ownership of the work itself rather than of the organisation the work 'belongs' with. Leaders are seen as colleagues and team leaders rather than as bureaucratic, controlling managers.

The characteristics of network processes in the 21st century are listed below.

- Professional relationships tend to be short-lived. Communication is distant – relationships by email only are common.

- 'Fuzziness' is replaced by an emphasis on interdisciplinary work and by encouraging relationships between unconnected areas in order to create something new.

- Nodes and links can today be defined as technology portals taking into account all the ICT and telecommunication infrastructures available to today's companies.

- Equality of importance of individuals is essential as there is more emphasis on team working.

- The importance of values has changed as there has been an increase in flexibility. The emphasis is now on the management of knowledge and therefore an increase in the sharing of information rather than pure self-interest.

Networking is seen as a major function of managing today and this is a role that is likely to change and develop over the next three to five years.

Creative management

Creative management can be defined as 'the quality of originality that leads to new ways of seeing and novel ideas. It is a thinking process associated with

89

imagination, insight, invention, innovation, ingenuity, intuition, inspiration and illumination.'[7] To understand something about creativity we need to know a little about its history. Creativity is said to have its origins in personality, natural talent, charisma or the association of interdisciplinary ideas. In addition, there are other theories that propose that creativity is caused by one of the following three factors: accident – a coincidence or a chance meeting that led to fortune and good ideas; genius and grace – caused by rare magical insights; or cognition – hard work and the application of intelligence.

Creativity can assist with managing complex organisational relationships by applying creative ideas and techniques. These would include straightforward methods of allowing employees freedom to try out new ideas and encouraging their own creativity in the workplace. Encouraging creativity to those who are working remotely implies a considerable degree of trust. Yet trusting staff to work outside the organisation in the first place can be viewed as empowering employees with a certain degree of responsibility. The rewards to managers for this degree of trust may be that the workforce is very committed; work may be completed at different times but the work may well be of a high standard and always completed on time. The organisation is viewed as a good, flexible employer; members of the organisation are happy and the organisation is able to recruit the best staff.

Another way in which creativity can help with managing organisational relationships is by changing the way in which people think so that, for example, there are more interdisciplinary ideas, which may lead to new inventions and eventually new products. There are many courses and books that teach people how to think and manage creatively, for instance, Edward de Bono's famous text on lateral thinking, which clearly demonstrates that anyone can be trained to think in a different way.[8]

An interesting study was completed in the early 1980s about two fascinating aspects of management.[9] The first was what senior managers think about (in a professional sense) and the second was concerned with how senior managers think. Briefly, the results showed that managers think about how to create effective organisational processes, how to deal with one or two main issues or about very general goals. Managers were found to think by using intuition, by tolerating ambiguity and by integrating action into the process of thinking – all concepts that are dealt with in the creativity literature. Creativity therefore can be seen to be a new cornerstone of managing complex organisational problems as it allows the freedom to work in new contexts and new environments. It is in no way restrained by structure, processes, functions or the nature of tasks; it is an unlimited resource, which is available to all with a little appropriate coaching.

Controlling the organisation – is it necessary?

Control can be defined within the context of an organisation as being about 'a process which helps to circumscribe idiosyncratic behaviours and keep them conformant to the rational plan of the organization…it is the function of control to bring about conformance to organizational requirements and achievements of the ultimate purpose of the organization'.[10] However, it could be argued that the key word is not control but context – if managers are managing people at a distance then they are not managing people who work within an organisation. This type of management requires new perceptions and ways of thinking, but it also requires a different view of control. The control process needs to be about providing support, encouraging collaborative work, setting clear goals and organising clear reporting structures, which are flexible and allow for the autonomy of the members of the organisation.

If managers are working in new as yet undefined contexts and individuals are not working directly within an organisation then this may imply that theories about behaviour in organisation may also need to be revisited. A classic behavioural study undertaken in the late 1950s made the following proposals.[11]

- Individuals need to be developed and socialized within appropriate culture (in order to fit into the traditional organisation).

- The organisation itself can be viewed as a strategy – a reason for completing a goal.

- Formal organisations are intended to be rational.

- Organisations should conform to the basic principles of scientific management – planning, organising, motivating and controlling.

How does this study of behaviour fit today's new patterns of working? The idea that individuals need to be developed in a particular way to fit into an organisation is probably no longer as valid as it used to be, although it is still important. If employees are working remotely the concept of fitting into a particular team of people is not vital. However, what is essential is the ability to work as a member of a team effectively, as many tasks now consist of project work. The second point remains unchanged – all organisations still have goals. It is questionable whether modern organisations are intended to be rational now that innovation and creativity are encouraged. The final point concerning organisations conforming to the principles of scientific management can still be applied, but in quite different ways, and probably using slightly 'softer' terms to describe functions, for example, designing, empowering, persuading and supporting (instead of planning, organising, motivating and controlling).

International perspectives

It is interesting to look at the problems of managing complex organisations from international perspectives. Some countries have unique cultures. In China organisations operate in a very formal, structured way, which makes changing the way in which workers are managed problematic. Management is associated with formal courtesies, with strict hierarchy, with folklore and traditions. Studies have shown that there is a need for new learning in developing operations in China.[12] However, China will maximise all opportunities – indeed the government has recently set up new 'economic zones' such as the city of Shenzen (just outside Hong Kong) to encourage enterprise and innovation in new businesses. Other developments such as those in Wuhan are taking place rapidly where many new business incubators are being developed. There is also an emphasis on the training of recent graduates to ensure that they are able to assist with the expansion of the newer industries.

Other countries such as Russia take a different view. They are caught up in the troubled marriage of east and west culture and so a radical change to work patterns and management style is difficult to implement. Although there is great emphasis placed on the encouragement of a form of western democracy for the former Soviet bloc there are many issues to be resolved. A major change in management style and flexible working practices may prove a little more difficult than, for example, places such as North America where freedom of speech and the ability to live one's life without undue interference from the state are highly valued assets. The controversy surrounding the sinking of the Kursk nuclear submarine on 11 August 2000 in the Barents Sea and the slow release of information from the relevant official bodies clearly demonstrated the difficulties of gaining accurate information quickly from reliable sources. Sometimes the results of a move to 'westernisation' seem strangely out of place. Examples are the huge banners advertising the American magazine *Newsweek*, which were prominently displayed during Autumn 2001 on the side of the building of the Palace of Culture in Warsaw, and the increasing number of fast-food retail outlets in old beautiful cities such as Budapest.

China and Russia are examples of countries that are keen to change but have inherent cultural problems to overcome if new working practices and management styles are to be accepted. Yet it has been suggested that nine trends or characteristics can be identified in organisations that are trying to blend one or more cultures.[13] These are:

- company spirit
- empowerment
- training
- team orientation
- co-ordination

- integration
- implicit behaviour norms
- customer focus
- a clear strategy.

These are all very positive factors, which will no doubt be identifiable in the organisations of many countries over a period of time.

The skills required to manage organisational relationships

The skills that are required for the manager to manage complex organisational relationships of the new working practices are good communication, development of networking skills, the ability to work in new contexts and the ability to perceive facts and issues in different ways. Other important assets are the 'softening' of the four management functions from planning, organizing, motivating and controlling to designing, encouraging, persuading and supporting.

A new understanding of the value of creativity and creative management is vital to take forward management as a discipline and to ensure continued effectiveness. Managers also need to develop analytical skills and to ask questions concerning whether the form of management and control they propose is suitable for the environment in which they operate.

References

1. Gee, C. and Burke, M.E. 'Realizing potential: the new motivation game', *Management Decision* 39(2), 2001, pp. 131–6

2. Fayol, H. *General and Industrial Management*. London: Pitman, 1949

3. Burns,T. and Stalker, G.M. *The Management of Innovation*. London: Tavistock, 1966

4. Vroom,V.H. and Yetton, P.W. *Leadership and Decision Making*. Pittsburgh: University of Pittsburgh Press, 1973

5. Kuhn, R.L. (ed). *Handbook for Creative and Innovative Managers*. New York: McGraw Hill, 1988

6. Lipnack, J. and Stamps, J. *Networking: the First Report and Directory*. New York: Doubleday, 1982

7. Henry, J. *Creative Management*. London: Open University in association with Sage, 1991

8. De Bono, E. *Lateral Thinking for Management*. Harmondsworth: Penguin, 1984

9. Isenberg, D.J. 'How senior managers think', *Harvard Business Review* 62(6), 1984, pp. 81–90

10. Tannenbaum, A.S. *Control in Organizations*. New York: McGraw Hill, 1968

11. Argyris, C. *Understanding Organizational Behaviour*. London: Tavistock, 1960

12. Lee, J.S.Y. 'Organizational learning in China', *Business Horizons* 42(1), Jan–Feb 1999, pp. 37–44

13. Fey, C.F. et al. 'Organizational culture in Russia – the secret to success', *Business Horizons* 42(6), Nov–Dec 1999, pp. 47–55

Chapter 7

Professionalism

Introduction

In 1998 seven key themes were identified that would impact on organisations in the 21st century.[1] These were:

- the humanising of work
- globalisation
- stakeholders and management
- sustainability
- high performance
- working across boundaries
- ethics and development in organisational life.

This final theme of ethics and development in organisational life is really about professionalism and although all the themes are important it is this particular issue that is one of the vital ingredients in a successful organisation and industry; this is the theme that this chapter will examine.

A profession can be defined as 'an occupation that involves knowledge and training in a branch of advanced learning'.[2] The use of the word profession implies a certain status, which originated from the fact that historically the term was, in general, associated with the medical and legal profession. Today, however, the term encompasses many types of work that require specialised skills. Use of the phrase 'a professional person' also implies expectancy of a certain level of behaviour and manners.

The aim of this chapter is simply to raise awareness of a few issues surrounding the concept of professionalism. This chapter will examine the relationship between professionalism, technology and new work patterns; professionalism and organisational stress; statements of ethics and professionalism, and the relationship between leadership and professionalism. This chapter ends with a discussion of skills that are required to manage this difficult area successfully.

Professionalism, technology and new work patterns

Professionalism is important because of the increasing use of technology in everyday work and the new work patterns that many organisations employ. These issues, combined with increasing globalisation of business, have meant that professionalism is a serious matter for all those employed in some form of organisation .

The way in which we communicate with colleagues both internally and externally is increasingly by remote methods such as telephone (land lines and mobile lines), text messages, fax and email. Email in particular brings with it a host of problems in the way in which communication is sent and received. As there is no allowance for voice tone, there can sometimes be an element of uncertainty in the understanding of vague messages of humour and irony. To counteract this various symbols have been devised, which help to ease the etiquette and sociability of email communication.

This technology etiquette is know as netiquette and certain symbols are now globally used, such as :-) to suggest humour and :-(to suggest sadness (sometimes used when making an apology). The increasing use of text messages through mobile phones has created another set of problems – many words and phrases are now abbreviated sometimes beyond all recognition – and potentially has the same problems as email communication. There is also the danger of simply making an error and sending the wrong messages to the wrong person. The impersonal nature of this form of communication creates a strong need for a shared sense of responsibility and a shared ownership of what is acceptable – a sense of what it is to be a professional at work. This is one of the reasons why guidelines that state definitions of professionalism are vitally important in today's organisations.

New work patterns have changed the essence of how we now regard work. The flexibility of working remotely, away from the office, has resulted in changes to communication as analysed above and changed the way in which we perceive our sense of belonging to an organisation. Gradually, the sense of belonging to the community of the organisation may fade, but it is very important that this is replaced by something else – a sense of shared values and beliefs, a sense of belonging to a profession rather than to a single organisation. As the structure of the organisation shifts and changes there needs to be some sense of stability and this can be provided by the concept of professionalism.

Zahra argued that there are certain requirements for a company to be successfully competitive in the 21st century.[3] These include visionary and dedicated leadership, the enhancement of corporate accountability, sustained investment, effective management of resources and the prudent use of assets to achieve growth. As organisations also become increasingly global it is no longer wise to deal only with local and national issues – the international arena is competitive and increasingly important if managers are to achieve an effective and efficient management style, and to act and react in a professional manner.

Professionalism and organisational stress

Professionalism can really only be developed if there is an organisational culture that encourages innovation and self-development, if employees consider that they are fulfilled in their working lives. A report by the International Association of Career Management Professionals (IACMP) concerning recent trends and issues in organisations found that many people are seeking to find four issues present in their working lives.[4] These are a clear sense of purpose, attention to personal goals, personal satisfaction and a congruence between work and personal goals. The survey showed that 'people are looking for leadership in today's workplace that includes integrity, an inspiring vision, and a compelling business strategy' – a true professional who will lead in a sensible, considerate and inspiring way.

However, the IACMP found that what happens in organisations is that, far from employees having job satisfaction and feeling fulfilled, tiredness and stress are frequent causes of complaint. The Association made the following recommendations to deal with these issues.

- Organisations should strive to be a model where stress among employees is minimised.
- Elements of increased employee control, an appreciative environment and opportunities for employees to innovate and create will aid in making the organisation a model of excellence.
- Organisations should strive to create an environment that is uplifting and non-threatening.
- Recognition of stress is important, as is knowing how to deal with it properly and effectively.
- The use of new technology and new tools such as life coaching and counselling techniques should be encouraged.
- There should be an understanding of diversity and multiculturalism.
- An effort should be made to change and adapt to the values of the 21st century rather than values of 20th century.

So, if organisations wish all employees to become professional in their outlook and behaviour they need first to attend to the issues listed above. In order to achieve this there is a need for effective management and the use of new and relevant management skills in order to allow this to happen, which will encourage the correct conditions for professionalism to grow, employees to develop and the organisation to be continually successful.

Statements of ethics and professionalism

Professional job attitudes are important. They are closely linked to what are known as ethics; ethics can be about morality, religion or a way of life, but are essentially about values and beliefs. It is these values and beliefs that form the basis of how people perceive the behaviour of a professional. This will vary, depending on circumstances, socialisation, gender and cultural beliefs. All employees, however, need to be accountable as organisations tend to be judged by actions and this, in turn, will reflect on the professionalism of the industry as a whole. It is now quite common for industries to form their own guidelines stating what they regard as a particular industry's professional issues and ethics. For example, one service-related group worked with the following headings in their guidelines on professionalism:[5]

- relationship to the public
- attention to work relationships
- professional development
- an awareness of professional attitudes.

This was used as a basic guideline for all staff and included as part of the induction programme for new staff joining the organisation. Many industries find this a useful starting point for the introduction of professionalism.

The relationship between leadership and professionalism

What is the relationship between leadership and professionalism? It can be seen as one where the leader exists simply to provide helpful guidance and provision of resources in order to assist organisational members to become professional. There are many theories of leadership but most theories can be categorised into three distinct schools of thought. The first is known as trait theory – where leaders are born, not made and all leaders have certain natural characteristics or traits, which result in a natural tendency to be the leaders in a group. However, some studies have shown that this is very difficult to prove.[6] The second is that of the leader in response to a situation – that different personalities will have a natural inclination to lead depending on the situation. The converse view of this theory is that it is difficult in organisations to have different leaders for every different situation. The third school of thought is that of the functional approach to leadership – where it is the content of leadership that is important, identifying the tasks that need to be completed and the practicalities of how to go about achieving the task. This is one of the most widely used concepts of leadership, although it can be seen as inflexible if the organisation does not change the functions of the leader when the functions of the organisation are altered. On the whole, however, this is one of the most popular and well-used theories of leadership.

In order to establish how these theories relate to the concept of professionalism we can attempt to examine each of them in turn.

- *Trait leadership theories* The concept of professionalism could be seen as 'inherently natural'. The leaders could be difficult to train to be professional as they may have a natural inclination to follow their own instinct and reactions.

- *Situational leadership* The concept of professionalism could emerge from a given situation. The training required to be professional is possible but could be difficult as different leaders emerge in different situations.

- *Functional leadership* The concept of professionalism would be a natural part of taking on the role of leader. Professional training would probably be an established part of the guidelines within the organisation.

Although all three types of leadership have some relationship to the concept of professionalism it is likely that functional leadership fits most closely with the idea of professionalism. It is also likely to exist in the type of organisation that is comparatively flexible and conducive to the implementation of flexible guidelines.

It has been argued[7] , however, that to compete and win in the competitive environment, organisational leaders need to move away from established management functions and focus on:

- using strategic vision to motivate and inspire
- empowering employees at all levels
- accumulating and sharing internal knowledge
- gathering and integrating external information
- challenging the status quo
- enabling creativity.

Most of these areas have been examined in some detail in previous chapters. They are, in fact, the very essence of what good management – and therefore true professionalism – is about.

Skills required in the management of professionalism

What skills are required to create, implement and manage the whole concept of professionalism? First, the ability to set up some kind of clear framework (if there is not already one in existence in the industry) that will allow employees to write and contribute to the provision of the final guidelines. It is essential that these are written with the team to ensure a sense of ownership. Openness with the team and respect for different views are essential characteristics of a manager.

Second, there must be an awareness of problems in an organisation and a willingness to alter the organisation to reduce stress for employees. This can be achieved by improving the organisational culture through concentration on areas such as flexibility, responsibility, standards, rewards and team commitment.[8]

Third, functional leadership provides the opportunity to be flexible, although both trait and situational leadership theories could be shaped around a kind of professionalism.

Professionalism was initially about adding value to the organisations but today it is about adding value to the person and the industry as a whole. It is important because it is intangible and difficult to measure – yet it is the one characteristic with which members of the organisation can establish their reputation and gain the respect of colleagues worldwide.

References

1. Murray, D. 'Seven development themes for the 21st century', *Organisations and People* 5(1), 1998, pp. 4–18

2. Hawkins, J.M. *The Oxford Paperback Dictionary*. Oxford: Oxford University Press, 1979

3. Zahra, S. 'The changing rules of global competitiveness in the 21st century', *Academy of Management Executive* 3(1), 1999, pp. 36–42

4. IACMP. *Changes in the World of Work: Fourth Report on Trends and Issues*. International Association of Career Management Professionals: Brighton, 2001

5. OALT. *Ontario Association of Library Technicians Statement of Ethics and Professionalism*. Ontario: OALT, 2001

6. Byrd, C. *Social Psychology*. London: Appelton-Century-Crofts, 1940

7. Dess, G. 'Changing roles: leadership in the 21st century', *Organisational Dynamics* 28(3), winter 2000, pp. 18–34

8. Watkins, C. 'How to improve organisational climate', *People Management* 7(13), 2001, pp. 52–3

Chapter 8

Putting it all together – skills summary

Introduction

This book has looked at the phenomenal power of business intelligence and the way in which management styles need to alter in order to manage organisations in this century successfully. We have discussed various subject areas pertinent to the running of a business by an organisation: the need to analyse the ever-changing external environment, to be aware of internal tensions and information flows, to link technology and business, to be flexible about business strategies, to be aware of the changing nature of marketing, to manage organisational relationships and the importance of professionalism.

The aim of this final chapter is to summarise the skills that managers need in order to be efficient and effective for the 21st century. This chapter also acts as a precursor for the case studies that follow and as an aide memoir for students who are revising this area for exams.

Skills summary

The analysis of the skills required by 'new' managers in each area can be summarised as follows.

Skills needed to deal effectively with the external environment:

- an awareness of change
- a capacity for reading widely
- alertness
- flexibility
- open-mindedness about work practices
- an ability to focus on the end game
- an ability to identify changes quickly
- an ability to plan reaction to changes
- an ability to implement plans
- an ability to re-evaluate situations in response to an ever-changing environment.

Skills needed to deal effectively with the internal environment:

- an ability to design structures which fit both the internal and external environment
- an ability to communicate effectively with the information systems team
- an ability to take on new roles as designers of organisational structures
- an ability to be flexible
- control of knowledge management
- astute powers of analysis
- an ability to manage within the constantly shifting patterns of organisations

- an ability to manage the internal environment in harmony with the external environment.

Skills needed to deal effectively with technology and business:

- skills of flexibility
- clarity of thought
- courage
- appreciation of team members' efforts
- skills of leadership.

Skills needed to deal effectively with business strategy:

- an ability to be objective
- an ability to think creatively
- an ability to think across levels
- an ability to develop new roles as a strategic option controller
- an ability to develop new roles as a knowledge management analyst.

Skills needed to deal effectively with the changing nature of marketing:

- technology skills
- knowledge of organisation structures
- knowledge of organisation roles
- information retrieval skills
- information collation skills
- an ability to be objective and alert to new ideas
- an ability to create new organisational patterns and practices
- awareness of the developing links between knowledge management and marketing.

Skills needed to manage organisational relationships:

- good communication skills
- development of networking skills
- an ability to work in new contexts
- an awareness of the 'softening' of the four management functions to designing, empowering, persuading and supporting
- an understanding of the value of creativity
- trust.

Skills related to professionalism:

- an ability to design a framework for guidelines
- openness with the team
- respect of different views
- an awareness of problems of stress in organisations
- a willingness to develop functional leadership skills.

Making a difference

If managers can create new roles and new methods of managing the future of organisations will be very exciting. Creativity and creative management are key skills in the 'new' manager's repertoire. Positive attitudes linked with an ability to be dynamic and a willingness to try out new ideas will ensure the success of both new and established business ventures.

It can be said that there are four major skills areas required of the 'new' manager and other skills are subordinate to these: people skills, the skill to deal with organisational issues, technology skills and resource skills. Sometimes more specific skills fit neatly into these categories, but sometimes skills overlap and belong to more than one group. These main skills areas are discussed below.

People skills

The first of the four most essential skills in this category is the development of networking skills by the manager and all the members of the organisation. By developing these skills the organisation is more likely to gain knowledge quickly of what the competition may be planning – and will grow stronger as a result of effective networking about products, service innovations and pricing strategies.

The second and third key skills are the ability to recognise the value of creativity in employees and to use creative ways of managing. If these are encouraged it will result in an innovative and forward thinking organisation.

Finally, it is important for the manager to be skilled in the 21st century functions of designing, empowering, persuading and supporting (rather than the classic functions of planning, organising, motivating and controlling). This will demonstrate a less controlling and a more encouraging management style. These functions are designed to allow members of the organisation more freedom to expand their roles, resulting in innovation and ultimately a more sustainable, profitable organisation.

The skill to deal with organisational issues

There are four key skills that can be identified as those needed by a 'new' manager in order to deal with organisational issues. The first is the ability to design successful organisational structures; a structure needs to take into account both the present and future needs of the business but also be flexible enough to take account of the constantly changing environment.

The second, third and fourth skills are all linked – they are astute powers of analysis, the ability to manage the constantly shifting patterns of the internal and external environment to ensure harmonisation, and the ability to think creatively across all levels of the organisation. The combination of these skills will assist the manager in dealing with complex situations within the organisation, improving organisational culture and ensuring that the organisation remains stable, but fluid enough to incorporate new ideas easily.

Technology skills

Five skills can be identified under this heading: the need for clarity of thought, the courage to undertake what can sometimes be massive investment in new technology, genuine appreciation of the work of team members, an awareness of the need for leadership skills and an understanding of technology. Sometimes organisations can be very complex and fragmented, which makes them difficult to manage. The ability to deal with these kinds of situations requires a logical and clear mind. Technology is constantly under development, with new products on the market almost every week – managers must make difficult decisions about upgrades to technology and this requires courage as well as knowledge of what is actually needed, now and in the future. Members of organisations who are involved with technology need to consider that their efforts and work are appreciated. Much of the work by IT specialists can be mundane and boring, yet it is often this work that keeps the system in good order and allows all its facilities to be fully exploited in the organisation. Finally, the 'new' manager should take into account the training needs of staff, be aware of the potential dip in productivity when staff are getting used to a new system, and be able to push a project through to completion.

Resource skills

When dealing with resource issues the two most important new skills are associated with knowledge management and business strategy. Within the area of knowledge management there are two roles of equal importance for the manager: to contribute to the role of the knowledge management controller and to contribute to the work of knowledge management analysis. This needs to be done in consultation with the knowledge management team and within the framework set up by the senior knowledge manager in the organisation.

Within the area of business strategy the manager needs to develop the skills of a strategic option controller, in order to be aware not only of all the choices but also of the implications and consequences of those choices. This will result in a more streamlined set of decisions being made over a period of time, decisions that have been considered in a logical way.

Additional skills

Good interpersonal skills are vital in an effective manager. However, in order to manage successfully in the 21st century it is important that certain additional key skills are developed. These are the ability to be open-minded, to focus on the end game, to be able to identify changes clearly and alter strategy accordingly, to re-evaluate situations and to communicate and listen effectively. A good manager must also be able to deal with competition by developing astute powers of analysis and a willingness to learn and develop as working patterns change.

Conclusion

One of the primary uses of information in organisations is to assist managers to make good quality, sound decisions. This can only be achieved by setting up effective information flows, taking into account present and future needs. It is also necessary to link the information available from the external environment with that of the internal environment in order to provide information about the competition and changing trends. All this can be achieved by the implementation of a good business strategy, which should be encouraged in line with the development of a marketing plan that takes into account how marketing is changing. It is also important to manage organisational relationships internally and structurally in a professional and successful way. While information and organisations are inextricably linked together, they are also connected with a third subject, that of management skills, and it is the connecting together of these three areas that has been discussed throughout this book.

The new skills discussed in this chapter also have implications for the training of present and future managers. The curricula of management and business-related courses need to be altered in accordance with new needs; this is done as a matter of course in most institutions but there should be flexibility in the style and mode of teaching in order to allow managers to try out new skills in a 'safe' environment. New types of information and communications technology should be used in order to develop managers to their true potential and to encourage a capacity for lifelong learning, as management styles will not remain static but will change over time. It is necessary to recognise changes that are taking place and to be willing to update and alter skills accordingly so that managers are always able to use relevant skills when needed.

The three case studies that follow can be used to illustrate points made in this book. Several questions are posed at the close of each case study and readers are encouraged to put their own additional questions; each case study is an entity in itself and many of the principles discussed above may be applied when considering them.

The Phenomenal Power of Business Intelligence

Case studies

Case study 1

Difficult days: difficult departments

(Anonymous)

Laura works at a small, specialist art college in a large manufacturing town. There are approximately 600 students, both full- and part-time. Laura works full-time as the manager of Student Services of the college and has responsibility for four members of staff – three full-time and one part-time. She is responsible herself to one of the two heads of faculty. Student Services exists to meet the needs of all the students, dealing with students' financial affairs, accommodation, problems completing work and personal matters.

The college is currently going through a period of change, which involves a reorganisation of the whole college and this affects all staff in some way. There has been much talk and some formal consultation, but no one seems to know what is going to happen and staff are worried about the security of their jobs. There are also rumours going around that the management at the 'top' will be changing, so the whole college is in turmoil.

Student Services is extremely busy and Laura has many pressures on her time. Because of this she finds that she has to organise her staff efficiently and frequently evaluate what they are doing. Although in theory she is responsible only to one head of faculty, in practice she also works closely with the other faculty head. This usually works well, but on occasions she feels pulled in different directions as sometimes she finds it difficult to prioritise her work in order to satisfy the demands made upon her. Each head of faculty naturally considers his request urgent.

Laura also has to liaise with external organisations as part of her daily work. She usually enjoys her work but often wishes that she didn't feel 'pulled in all directions'. She is currently experiencing difficulties in dealing with the staff for whom she is directly responsible.

Sally is one of the full-time members of Laura's team and she seems to be permanently miserable and often snaps at colleagues and also at students who come in to use the service. She is near to retirement and has worked at the college for over 25 years. The quality of her work is excellent and she pays a lot of attention to detail, making her an asset, but with her recent behaviour, Laura is beginning to despair.

Robert is also full-time and generally gets on well with the students. He is the counsellor for the college. His paperwork is sometimes lacking. He often 'disappears' from the office for long periods of time, which causes a strain on the remaining members of staff. No one has challenged him on his disappearances, which seem to be increasing in frequency.

The third full-timer, Joan, is good at her job but often appears to be the cause of regular upsets concerning other members of staff, both in the college and among her immediate colleagues. She maintains that the management does not keep the staff informed of what is happening and feels undervalued. She appears sometimes to elaborate facts and often keeps information to herself when Laura feels that she could be more open and share things.

The final and newest team member, Anna, works part-time hours. She has a young family and provides reception and backup secretarial work to the rest of the team. Laura is pleased with the work of the recently recruited young woman, but suspects that she is already looking for better paid work elsewhere.

The members of the Student Services all try to meet once a week but because of pressures of time and appointments meetings usually occur nearer to once a month, with Laura 'snatching' the odd moment to tell staff what is happening. As a result of this, Sally, Robert and Joan feel overworked and not valued enough as staff members.

A typical day at the college for Laura, Robert, Joan, Sally and Anna consists of seeing students by appointment or informally, with one hour for lunch. They often do not have the time to complete paperwork as thoroughly as they would like, nor to talk to each other, and as it is so busy they resent the fact that Robert disappears so often. Joan is also often a source of annoyance as she has the knack of 'winding everyone up', with the result that staff often go home feeling stressed.

Questions

1.   Would the introduction of new working patterns solve any of Laura's problems?

2.   Do you consider that the management control mechanisms are appropriate for the environment? Identify any changes that you think would help the department to run more efficiently.

3.   Could aspects of creative management be introduced into this situation? What do you consider would be the results of this kind of approach?

Case study 2

School problems

(Anonymous)

Paul arrived at school as usual at 8.15 a.m. and stared at the mountain of work piled high on his desk. Year 9 lower set Maths books (there wouldn't be too much to mark there) sat next to Year 7 top set Maths books, which sat next to the exam papers from two years ago. The Year 11 pupils had attempted these last week but they had still not been corrected. Yet overshadowing all this were the mental stresses and strains introduced by his new responsibilities. Life at St John's School used to be so simple. Under the guidance of the highly organised Alistair Gray, the Maths Department ran like clockwork. Paul was a small, but vital, cog in the wheel. He always marked his books puncutally. He never felt flustered. He was happy in his little world of simultaneous equations and geometric theorems. What had led him to volunteer to oversee the workings of the new computing suite? Was it pure ambition, or merely insanity?

At first it didn't seem too bad, but now he felt very gullible. Without doubt he was being exploited. He had believed the assurances that his teaching load would be lightened although, with the staffing available, he couldn't see how this could be possible. Still, if Mrs Wilkinson, an experienced and trusted headmistress, said it could be done, then surely he should believe her. Now, on this dull, wet November morning, Paul saw clearly that it could not be done.

It appeared to Paul that he was paying the price for his interest in computers and all things to do with them. He wished he hadn't aired his knowledge so freely around school. Now it was his fault that the suite wasn't functioning to full capacity and that, according to Miss Phillips, the Business Studies candidates' chances of GCSE success were already in jeopardy. It was his fault that Mr Blackburn's brilliantly composed scheme of work for lower school Information and Communications Technology had failed to take off. It was, so claimed Mrs Fleming from the Humanities Department, Paul's fault that the Key Stage 3 pupils' map reading and atlas skills were undeveloped owing to a lack of suitably programmed machines. Paul was sure that when he was at school maps were printed on paper.

As the rain began to hammer ever harder against his window, Paul felt his frustration welling up inside him far more vigorously than it had done previously. Why didn't Miss Phillips concentrate on those aspects of the scheme of work that didn't involve Information and Communications Technology? Was Mrs Fleming seriously suggesting that adolescents' geographical skills couldn't be developed in an ordinary classroom? (Perhaps she wasn't up to the job of teaching the pupils without the aid of complicated machinery?) Was Paul himself prepared to receive Blackburn's constant and vitriolic tongue-lashings? The man seemed to be waging some kind of personal vendetta against him and, Paul decided, it just wasn't on. He was doing his best. It wasn't his fault that GFK was delaying in ensuring the system was correctly installed.

He strode purposefully down the corridor and rapped vigorously on Mrs Wilkinson's door. There were two lights next to the frame: if the green lit up, you were privileged to be able to see the headmistress, but if the red was illuminated then clearly the time was not right. This impersonal touch infuriated Paul at this best of times, and this was not the best of times. Today it only served to heighten his anger, as did the seemingly interminable delay during which neither light shone.

He knocked again. The green light came on. Agitated, Paul entered.

'This new role of mine...', began Paul, but he was stopped in his tracks by Mrs Wilkinson's outstretched hand.

'Paul,' she said calmly. 'I know we have been having problems with GFK. I've rung them myself on several occasions. [Had she?] But I think you have to realise that whereas the school is my responsibility, I have to delegate tasks to my tried and trusted staff. You're the computing man. You're the expert. The system's your baby.'

'You're quite right, I am the computing man. I am the expert. But, as you say, I am not in charge of everything. I am tired of being blamed for virtually everything round here. I can't do right for doing wrong. My head of department has been urging me to solve the system's problems, yet when I was a few minutes late to class after phoning the computer company at break the other day, he was livid. Coming down here now I passed Bob Atkinson on his way to science. His look told me exactly what he thought of me. Everywhere I turn I face enmity and resentment and I would like to know what you, as head, are going to do about my intolerable working conditions.'

Unfortunately, Mrs Wilkinson's curt response, which offered no new assurances, meant that, at least for that wet and miserable November morning at St John's, there was an absentee in the Maths Department. The problem of the under-trained staff seemed no nearer a solution and would undoubtedly escalate if not addressed very soon.

Questions

1.   As a 21st century manager putting your 'new' skills into practice how would you resolve this situation?

2.   In what way is professionalism a relevant concept to the above case study?

3.   Analyse the implementation and management of the computing suite.

Case study 3

The high price of fashion

(Anonymous)

This case study demonstrates the tensions between management and customers in the retail industry, the management being the supplier of the goods and the customer the high street retailer.

All suppliers had exhibited their new lines at the Paris fashion show, resulting in orders for a new range of embroidered dresses. The customer requested that a new line of embroidered dresses (in a ratio of sizes 12 to 18) be in stock for a specific date.

A critical path was raised by the supplier allowing a period of two weeks as an extra safety net. [A critical path is a way of showing all the steps that need to be taken to ensure a specific target date is met.] The critical path was submitted to management for approval; management removed the two week safety net that the production department had included, saying that it had to show that the supplier was sharper than the competitors and therefore needed to be in stock by an earlier date. The adjusted critical path was then submitted to the customer who was happy with the date set.

Initial samples were made of the new dresses, which then had to be submitted to the customer's buying department of the customer for final approval. This took much longer than expected, so much so that the department changed the agreed dates set out on the original critical path.

However, the buying department did not inform its relevant colleagues (merchandisers) who would organise the logistics of the goods being delivered to store, even though they were only a desk apart. When the buyer finally agreed on the modifications of the embroidery for the dresses two weeks had elapsed. The implications of this were that the production department knew they needed to submit a revised critical path, giving a later date of two weeks from that originally set (the two week safety net having been removed by management at the start). However, the merchandisers had informed the shops that they would be receiving the new dresses on a certain date, and had adjusted space in the stores and shelving accordingly.

The situation was now thus: the production department needed to put pressure on the outside embroiderer to produce goods by an earlier date than agreed, and to produce a slightly different product than agreed.

The goods were ordered electronically by the customer from the supplier, the procedure being that the customer was informed of the number of dresses that were in stock on a Thursday, and the dresses were requested electronically from the supplier on the following Monday. Each shop belonging to the customer was allocated a certain number of dresses, and corresponding space on a specific lorry was organised.

On the Thursday the goods were due to be in stock, the embroiderer did not have the goods ready. The following course of action was taken by the production department in agreement with management and the reluctant agreement of the embroiderer.

A certain number of goods were declared as being in stock to the customer on the Thursday; although these totalled the quantity required by the customer, the dress sizes declared were not in the ratio the customer requested – there were no size 18s. The embroiderer worked overtime at the weekend, and the goods were picked up by the supplier's production department early on Monday morning; these goods then needed to be scanned and checked. This procedure took until midday on Monday.

The administrative implication of not having the goods in stock at the supplier on the Monday morning was that the goods were not listed as being available at the supplier, therefore the appropriate computer-generated packing note was not produced. The warehouse was not able to start packing goods for the retailer until goods were scanned into the supplier's computer system, and the packing note produced. This note also itemised the specific bays from which to take the stock.

Although the goods did get loaded onto the relevant transport, the transport was held up for several hours waiting for all these procedures to take place. However, the customer was happy that the goods had been declared on time, and picked up in time to be delivered to the relevant shops. And so, the high street retailer could at last sell 'Paris fashions', although the problems with the ordering system had been rather a high price to pay.

Questions

1.   What problems can you identify with the way in which this situation was dealt with by the management?

2.   What skills would you recommend the suppliers need to develop in order to prevent a similar situation recurring in the future?

3.   Do you consider that the whole ordering procedure could be simplified and if so in what way? What would be the skills implications of your new ordering procedure?

Index